GAMES MASTER
PRESENTS

P9-DNN-595

THE ULTIMATE
BUILDER'S GUIDE
IN MINECRAFT

BECOME A MINECRAFT MASTER BUILDER!

SCHOLASTIC INC.

CREATIVE DIRECTOR
Mark Donald

EDITOR
William Salmon

WRITERS
Louise Blain, Wesley Copeland, Aiden Dalby,
Emma Davies, Matthew Gilman, Ford James,
Danielle Lucas, Jen Simpkins, James Nouch,
Robin Valentine, Ben Wilson, Mark Wynne

LEAD DESIGNER
Adam Markiewicz

DESIGNERS
Emma Birch, Andy Downes, Ali Innes,
Jamie Orrell, Emma Swift

PRODUCTION
Rob Mead-Green

ISBN: 978-1-338-59471-3

10 9 8 7 6 5 4 3 2 1   19 20 21 22 23

Printed in the U.S.A. 40
First edition, September 2019

WELCOME TO
THE ULTIMATE BUILDER'S GUIDE IN MINECRAFT

There are no limits to what you can make in Minecraft! It's been designed to give you everything you need to let your imagination run wild and build truly spectacular creations! But maybe you want a helping hand, or a few ideas and suggestions . . . That's where this book comes in. From ancient castles to sinister sea monsters, you'll find lots and lots of builds for makers of every skill level. There are also hints, tips, and a handy glossary to explain what the different terms mean. If you're a noob, then this book will make you a master builder in no time. And if you're already super-skilled, then it will give you loads of great new ideas. Now, what are you waiting for? Turn the page, get building, and have fun!

CONTENTS

Welcome to your Minecraft builder's guide! We'll have lots of fun.

BUILDS

TIPS

FEATURES

ESSENTIALS

ESSENTIAL BLOCKS

The blocks that every builder needs to fill their chests with and what you can do with them . . .

Blocks are the very foundation of Minecraft—you mine them to collect resources, build cool structures with them, and use them to craft new materials and tools to play with. Simply put, without blocks, there would be no Minecraft at all! Here we'll take you through the most useful blocks, explain why you need them, and describe some of the exciting projects you can do with them.

WOOD

It may not be spectacular, but you won't get very far in Minecraft without wood. Not only do you need it to craft important tools like pickaxes and torches, wood is also used to build crafting tables, which will open up a whole new world of crafting possibilities.

STONE

When you want to start building permanent shelters in Minecraft, you'll need to get something sturdy that will hold up against hazards like creepers and fire. Stone will do the trick. You'll also need it to make a furnace for smelting iron, steel, and other materials.

OBSIDIAN

If you want to get to the Nether to collect the exclusive items that can be found there, you'll need to craft a portal. For that you need obsidian. It's also an ingredient for cool blocks that will increase your power, such as beacons and enchanting tables.

REDSTONE

Redstone acts like a wire, allowing you to make cool mechanical devices like trains, automatic doors, lights that can be turned on and off, clocks, and almost anything else you can think of. Minecraft wouldn't be half as fun without it.

DIAMOND

Once you've been playing Minecraft a while, you'll want something sturdier than standard tools. With diamond, you can craft pickaxes, swords, and axes that will last for ages. You'll also want to craft yourself diamond armor to protect yourself from tough mobs.

BEACON

Get some obsidian, glass, and a nether star and you can cast the awesome beacon block. These blocks can be used to shoot a beam of light into the sky so you can always find an important location and to give you status buffs like increased speed and strength.

10 TIPS FOR A BETTER BUILDING IN... MINECRAFT

Give your Minecraft builds a boost with these top tips . . .

1

QUICK WALLS

Building a wall? Don't go from side to side, go up and down instead. The quickest way to create massive structures in Creative mode is to hold down the "Place/Use" button and "Jump" button to build upward, and to build in the opposite direction. The game will repeat the process and make the wall quickly!

Good

Bad

2

PERFECT WINDOWS

Windows always look better with depth. So, the next time you're adding in a window frame, try placing the glass blocks or panes one block behind the actual frame. And if you decide to use panes instead of blocks, it's easier to place the panes onto already laid blocks rather than on top of one another.

Good

Bad

3

MIX IT UP A BIT

Vary your building materials all the time. Using stone for an entire house is fine, but mixing it up always ends up looking better. Why not use wood for the roof and planks for the walls? Have you tried chopping out each corner and replacing it with wood? Give it a try.

Good

Bad

4

POINTY ROOFS

Build roofs, not pyramids. When you've created the main walls of a home, it's easier to think you should run steps all around the outside to create a roof. Don't. You'll end up with a pyramid. Instead, build a step formation going up, then build the roof back from there.

Good

Bad

5

MAKING TURRETS

If you're planning on building a castle turret, always use odd numbers for the circular base. Whenever you create a tower or castle turret, make sure the very bottom, before building it up, has odd-numbered main lengths. If they're even numbers, you won't end up with that lovely spike at the top of the spire.

Good

Bad

Don't be a blockhead! Read our top tips for better Minecraft builds!

Hey, horse! Do you know what it means if you find a horseshoe?

Yeah . . . It means one of my friends is walking around in his socks!

6

PAPER PLANS

Ever tried making pixel art from a picture you found online? The reason that works is because you're working from a plan. The same logic applies to everything in Minecraft. Draw some ideas to get a rough idea of size. It doesn't have to look perfect on paper, but it helps to know what you roughly should be doing.

7

GREENERY IS GOOD

Scenery is as important to your build as block choice. Adding hedges (rows of leaf blocks), a nice garden, or a mini farm helps breathe life into your builds. Similarly, pathways, too, help to break up the boring green of the surrounding area. Go on . . . make your world look great!

TAKE YOUR TIME

Don't rush. Seriously, try your hardest not to be impatient. A build that takes three hours will always look better than one that's rushed out in 30 minutes. The worst mistake any builder can make is rushing. Rushing leads to mistakes, and mistakes are what you don't want. Enjoy the build experience!

Good

Bad

RUN A TEST

Test in superflat—build in regular worlds. Although clearing out land for a build on premade worlds can be time consuming, the surrounding landscape—mountains, ravines, lakes, villages – means your builds will always be surrounded by something, rather than in superflat, where the world seems empty.

USE YOUR WORLD

If you're making something big for the first time, consider using your surroundings to help you build. If a castle lookout post seems like it's too difficult, try building it into the side of a mountain. That way you only need to build half, and you've got the option of building rooms inside of the mountain.

Let's build it!
BUNK BEDS!

These bunk beds are perfect for a Minecraft sleepover . . .

I'm definitely getting the top bunk for our Minecraft sleepover!

INFO

BUNK BEDS
Difficulty:
NORMAL
Nothing too tricky here, but great for sleepovers!
Time needed:
20 MINS

START HERE

1 **LET'S KICK-START** this bunk bed build by creating a three-high wall that's five blocks across out of black wool. This smaller section is going to act as the back of our bunk beds. Feel free to place it wherever you want, but for the sake of simplicity, we placed it in the corner of a room.

2 **WITH THE** back side of your beds laid down we can now start work on one of the sides. Looking directly at the front of the wall you just built, aim your eyes to the left and extend the wall so that it comes out by two blocks, again making this from black wool.

□ Creative △ Inventory

3 **TO THE** right of the jutting-out section, drop down two more wool blocks coming from the back wall. After that, place one single block of purpur on top of the farthest back block, then add in some purpur steps in front of the purpur block and in front of the wool blocks.

Creative ▢ Inventory △

4 **NEXT GRAB** some beds and stand on top of the purpur blocks. Look to the right and lay down two beds next to one another on the ground. Make sure that the pillow area is two blocks away from you so whoever sleeps in the top bunk doesn't accidentally step on your head.

5 NOW WE'RE going to need to make a giant slab to hold the top bunk bed in place. Grab some purpur half slabs and connect them to the single purpur block and the set of steps next to it. This should look like a mini small roof over the two beds. This will carry the next beds in our project.

Inventory   L2 Sleep   R2 Mine

Creative   Inventory

6 YOUR BUNK beds should now be starting to take shape, so let's add two more beds on top of the purpur half slabs. As with the last beds, it's best to keep them facing the same way to mirror the bottom bunk and, again, to avoid any accidental head-smushing.

7 **GRAB YOUR** trusty black wool again and let's finish off the sides of the bunks. Look to where the back black wool pokes out to the right of the beds. From here, build another three-high wall. Basically, we're repeating what we did in Step 2, only on the farthest right-hand side.

8 **NOW FOR** some finishing decorations. Head into the menu and grab some purpur half slabs. See how the black wool creates a kind of C shape around the bunks? Simply run a row of slabs around the top of the bunks. Doing so definitely helps to break up all the black.

BUILD THIS!

> I'd better warn you, I snore in bed!

9 **TO FINISH** up this build, we're going to add some drawers to the bunks. To do this, place two item frames on both sides of the bottom bunk. Then all that's left is to fill them with wooden buttons and they should end up looking like drawers full of toys. Now you can jump into bed!

BEFORE
– Just a regular fireplace?

AFTER
– Opens to a secret room!

INFO

SECRET FIREPLACE
Difficulty:
HARD
REDSTONE IS TRICKY STUFF; YOU NEED TO FOLLOW CLOSELY!

Time needed:
1¾ HOURS

EXTRA INFO:
This is a good build to do before you build a mansion house.

BUILD A SECRET FIREPLACE

Hide a special room behind the fireplace in a Minecraft house using redstone!

The power of fire always amazes! This turns into a doorway!

Minecraft gets really tricky when you start messing around with redstone! Think of it like an electrical circuit that you can wire up to do whatever you want. In this feature, we will show you how to use the different blocks of redstone to create a fireplace in your house that will move to one side, revealing the entrance to a secret room where you can store all of your most precious possessions!

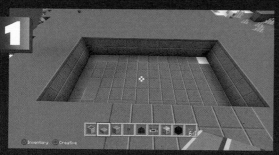

CLEAR THE WAY

Start off by finding a nice, big open area in your world to start your build. (Remember it's much quicker to burn down trees and use water buckets to clear away shrubs.) Next, build a big old 12x6 hole that's two blocks deep.

LOAD UP YOUR HOTBAR

Add a stone brick, stone half slab, sticky piston, redstone torch, redstone dust, redstone repeater, dispenser, nether brick, and fire charges to your hotbar. Then place two sticky pistons facing up with stone bricks on top.

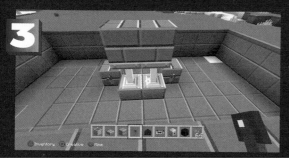

CHECK YOUR REDSTONE

It's worth mentioning here before we go on, with redstone builds it's important you triple-check everything. With that in mind, one block diagonally behind the sticky pistons, place two blocks of stone bricks with a redstone torch on each.

AROUND THE BACK

Head around to the back of the build. On the left-hand side, place a redstone repeater facing outward. Do the same for the block on the right. Then using redstone dust, run a line of two in between the blocks.

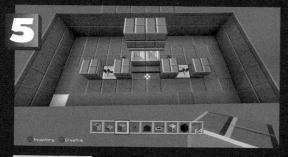

LINE IT UP

Get your stone bricks out again and place one block of stone brick on the far left, next to the repeater. Next place a stone brick block on the far right side. At this point, everything should be lining up symmetrically.

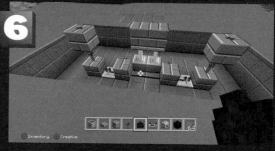

BALANCING TORCHES

On each of the two blocks you placed, put a redstone torch directly on top. Then on top of the torches, place a single stone brick. To finish, grab your redstone dust and drop a piece on top of each new block.

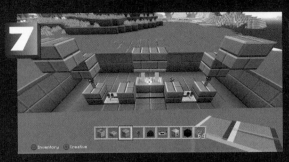

MORE BRICKS

This next part of the build is nice and simple. Diagonally up and one block out from the blocks with redstone dust on, place in another stone brick coming off on both sides. And remember, it all has to be symmetrical.

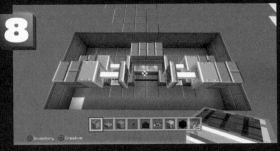

STICKY PISTON FUN

Now we're going to add in some sticky pistons, four to be exact. On the inside of the last two blocks you placed, add an inward-facing sticky piston. Then add two more on the redstone dust blocks, again, making sure that these are facing inward.

ADD FIRE CHARGES

Go around to the front side of the contraption you're building. Everything still symmetrical? Good. On top of each of the lower sticky pistons, place two dispensers on either side facing inward, and fill them with fire charges.

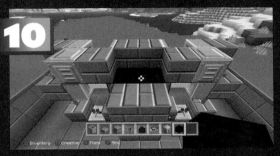

USING NETHER BRICKS

Place nether brick in between both of the extended lower pistons. Go one block up from there and place two blocks behind and one on both sides. (The blocks on the side carry the fire charge needed for relighting the fire.)

ADDING A SWITCH

That's the main bulk of this section out of the way. For our on/off switch, head to the base of the structure. Put a brick coming off the block with a torch on it, then place a sticky piston behind it, and a redstone torch in the floor.

MORE WIRING UP

Behind the sticky piston, place down a repeater going into it. Then, behind the repeater, place a regular piston one block into the floor. And finally, place one block of sand on top of the piston. This is looking good, and we're almost there now!

13

REPEATERS REPEATING

Place three blocks of stone bricks forming a reverse L-shape behind the sand block, so it's like a mini step. On top of the first block, drop down a redstone repeater. On the block one up from that, dust it with redstone.

14

TEST THE OPENING

Drop a block above the dust and put a button on its face. You should now be able to press the button and watch as your fireplace magically opens. Press the button again, and it'll close and relight itself. Pretty cool, right?

REDSTONE TIPS

THERE ARE lots of ways that you can obtain redstone. The most common is by mining redstone ore and smelting it down using any fuel you like. You can also kill a witch (they often drop redstone dust when they die), or trade it with villagers. You can break redstone with pretty much anything from your fists to the best weapons.

BREWING, CRAFTING and circuits all use redstone. For example, making a mundane potion is done with redstone and a water bottle. Mundane potions are then used to go on and create more exciting potions! Then crafting many potions with redstone will increase their duration, although with some, it will decrease the level.

MANY OBJECTS need redstone in their crafting ingredients to work. A clock is made with redstone and four blocks of gold; a compass is redstone and four blocks of iron ingot; a piston is redstone with three wood planks, four cobblestone and an iron ingot; and a redstone torch is redstone and a stick.

WHEN MAKING redstone circuits, it's important to know that the power redstone dust can carry gets weaker the farther away from the power source it goes. The maximum distance is 15 blocks. If you need to go farther you will have to add redstone repeaters to your circuit to boost power levels back to 15.

15

BUILD THE FIREPLACE

Replace the button stone with gray-glazed terracotta to look like wallpaper. Then run two more next to it, count four blocks, then add another three. In the center, we'll now begin to make what will become our fireplace surround.

16

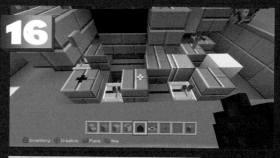

MORE REDSTONE WIRING

For the inside button, place a second redstone torch in the center at the bottom next to the other, a repeater in front of the right-side block, and a dusted block behind the repeater. Lastly, drop a block above the dust with a button on.

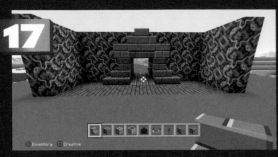

MAKING WALLS

Now head back to the front of the contraption and build a walkway going through the middle. Build the glazed terracotta walls up, change the floor for wooden planks, and then create a fireplace out of stone bricks and stone steps.

THE SECRET ROOM

But where does the fireplace lead to? How about adding a spiral door with a secret room? That sounds good. Head to the end of the walkway and dig a five-deep, 7x6 hole. Place some stone bricks in the formation seen in the image above.

A SPIRAL EFFECT

Head to the other side of the would-be door. Now with sticky pistons, place four as they are in the image above. The blocks that they're attached to will be the blocks that move to create a spiral effect which will wow your friends!

MORE STONE BRICKS

Go back around the front of the fire and look at the piston that is now on your left. Now drop a stone brick below it, and one block diagonally underneath. The gap behind the last block is where you go for the next step.

PLACING PISTONS

Below the first stone brick from Step 20, place a downward sticky piston with a block of redstone below it, a repeater to the right, a stone brick to the right of that, then another sticky piston facing up on top of the brick.

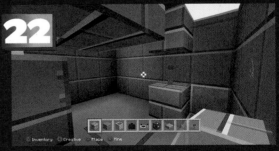

IS REDSTONE WEIRD?

Behind the stone brick on the right, create an L out of redstone dust leading into another brick with a redstone torch on. Above that torch, place yet another block with another redstone torch on. Yes, redstone IS really weird.

23

WATCH YOUR TICKS

Place a block with some redstone dust on it above the redstone torch. Drop a block to the left with a west-facing, two-tick repeater on. To finish this step, next drop some more redstone dust on the block to the left.

24

NEARLY THERE

Look at the front of the door. On the western two blocks, add a single stone brick on the upper side. Place a redstone torch underneath on the wall, then a button on the opposite side of the block, and you're all finished!

25

WHAT WILL YOU HIDE?

You can build whatever you want on the other side of the door. If you've got lots of epic loot you don't want people messing with, this is a great place to keep it. But we think that iron blocks make for a great little bank vault!

26

DECORATE YOUR ROOM

To round this build out, bring your walls back around onto themselves, add in a door, decorate the floor with a nice carpet, and add in windows. Now go forth and amaze your friends with the greatest secret fireplace room they've ever seen!

Your friends will be amazed when you show them the secret room behind the fire!

Let's build it!
A SECRET WALL

A secret wall entrance may come in very handy!

Where is the secret entrance? If i told you, it wouldn't be secret!

INFO

SECRET WALL
Difficulty:
NORMAL
Quite a simple build, but may be very useful . . .
Time needed:
30 MINS

START HERE

1 **FIRST THINGS** first, pull out some stone and sticky pistons. Lay down six stone blocks all in a long row and knock out the middle two blocks. Next, on the left side, create an L shape out of sticky pistons. After that, head to the right and do the same but in reverse.

2 **PLACE YOUR** wall blocks in front of the sticky pistons. We're using gold blocks here to show you where they should go, but if your wall is going to be made of stone, use stone blocks instead. After that, run a row of stone blocks across the top front to create an archway.

3 **THE NEXT** thing we need to do is build a roof on top of our device so we can lay down redstone. Coming from the row above the doorframe, add in another two rows behind it. You can now go ahead and add redstone repeaters and redstone dust to your hotbar.

4 **ONE BLOCK** in from both sides, place down redstone repeaters facing outward. This next part is important: Hit each of them once so they're both on two ticks. If you don't, the wall will push the wrong parts out. Next dust in the redstone in between and around, as shown.

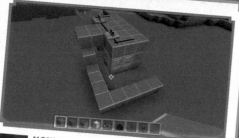

5 NOW IT'S time to add in somewhere for our lever to go. Add in four blocks behind the redstone dust. Next, add a step down, build it four blocks out, then four to the right. Do not build the arm too close to the pistons as it'll accidentally activate them, and we really don't want that.

6 LOOKING FROM the back, connect the redstone dust on the right (in between the repeaters) down and along the stone arm. One block after the steps, drop in a repeater facing the steps. At the end of the arm, add another block with a lever on its face.

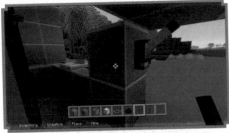

7 GO ON. You know you want to. Pull the lever and marvel at our really simple, really compact, redstone secret wall. If you're looking to add a lever on the inside, place one on the back of the step you made leading to the lever. That way you can close the wall behind you.

8 IF YOU'RE creating this out in the open, now's a good time to build up the walls around it. Do keep in mind you don't want to place blocks directly on top of the redstone as it will disrupt the circuit. So be sure to build the walls a few blocks taller to avoid any issues.

BUILD THIS!

> I read a book once. Green, it was.

9 YOUR SECRET wall can be placed anywhere, and can lead to whatever you want. Why not try building a library with a hidden bookcase entrance to a loot room? Or why stop at a loot room? Build the door into a mountain, then you'll have the space to create an entire house behind it!

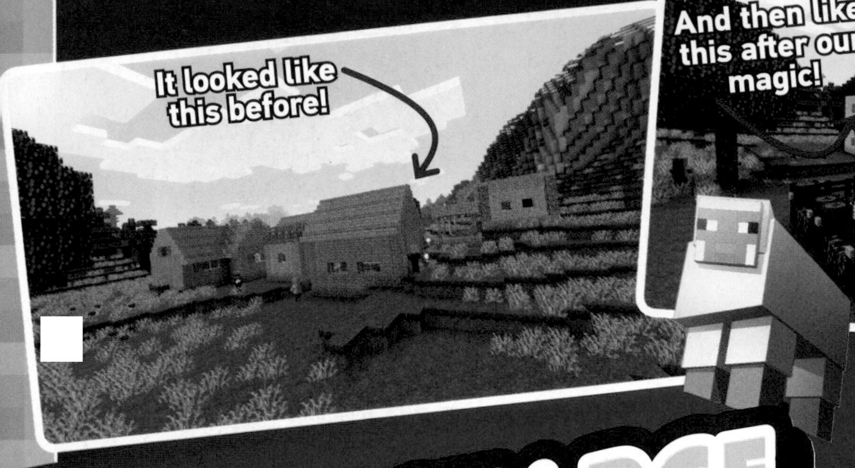
It looked like this before!

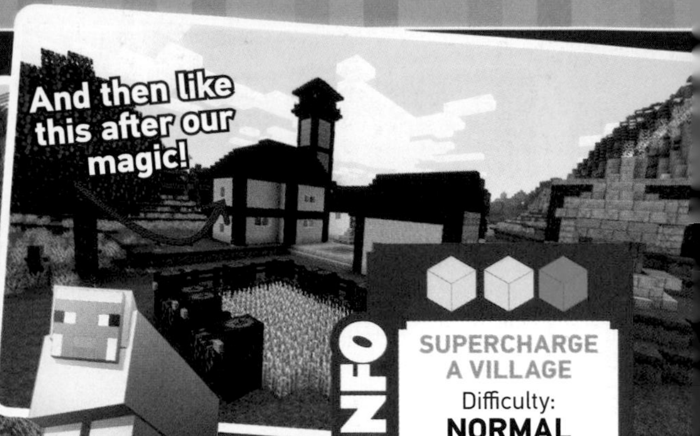
And then like this after our magic!

INFO

SUPERCHARGE A VILLAGE

Difficulty:
NORMAL
WITH A BIT OF TIME AND PATIENCE, EVERYONE CAN DO THIS

Time needed:
2½ HOURS

EXTRA INFO:
You can choose your own stone and wood blocks if you like.

SUPERCHARGE A VILLAGE

Villages might naturally spawn, but they're not naturally attractive. We show you how to remodel them into something fantastic!

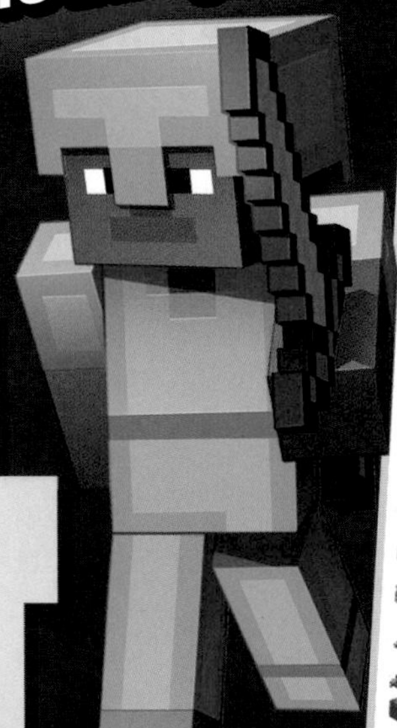

Load your Hotbar with...

- Cobblestone
- Stone Bricks
- Stone Brick Stairs
- Stone Half Slabs
- Lava Bucket
- White Terracotta
- Dark Oak Wood
- Dark Oak Planks
- Dark Oak Wood Stairs
- Cracked Stone Bricks
- Glass Panes
- Cobweb
- Water
- Cobblestone Wall
- Leaves
- Hoe
- Wheat
- Stone Buttons
- Armor Stand
- Torches

When you create a new world in Minecraft, villages will naturally spawn in a random way in desert, taiga, savanna, and plains biomes. Each biome will create a village in its own style, but none of them are that attractive. We're going to show you ways to demolish and rebuild key parts of your chosen village—improve the blacksmith's forge, sort out those pesky Iron Golem—and supercharge your village!

1

SEARCH FOR A VILLAGE

Find yourself a lovely village that's ripe for a makeover. Chances are when you find one the ground there is going to be a mess, so let's kick things off by mining up all the grass and dirt in between all the buildings so we have a nice flat surface to work with.

2

GRAB SOME STONE

Arm yourself with some cobblestone and stone bricks. We're using the City texture pack on the PlayStation 4, but use whichever pack you like. Run the stone bricks around the outside edge of the pathway area. In the middle lay down some cobblestone.

3

FIND THE BLACKSMITH

Head to where the blacksmith's forge has spawned inside your village. Every village is unique, so where it will be will likely be different from ours. Once you've found it, smash up the forge, mine up the roof, and clear the space out so all you're left with is the ground.

4

CHARGE THAT HOTBAR

Add some stone stairs to your hotbar and create a 4x4 square with them. Knock out each of the corners, then head to the front side and mine that up, too. With stone stairs in hand, run a row of outward-facing stairs next to one another.

5

STONE BRICKS

You should be left with three solid stone brick rows and one row of stairs. Look toward the stone brick rows. Ignoring the middle block on each side, place down stone stairs facing outward on each of the ends. Fill in the middle of the stairs with stone bricks.

6

REBUILDING WORK

On each of the middle blocks you just placed down, add another set of stairs facing away on top of the structure. Next to each step, on the side, lay down stone bricks. When you view from above, it should look like you're filling in the inside corners.

7

KEEP BUILDING UP

Your new blacksmith's forge will be looking a little bit weird at the moment. Don't worry, it's not finished. Looking to the four stone bricks from the last step, drop stairs on top of them and connect them so you're left with a cross shape on top.

8

A SMASHING TIME

Next, we're going to mine up those four corner stairs. Head inside the blacksmith's forge, and when you've worked out which blocks are the four inside corners, smash them to bits. You should end up with a gap from where they were. Cover that with stone half slabs.

9

WATCH OUT—LAVA!

Grab a lava bucket and fill in the bottom. Then with stone bricks, create a chimney poking out of the cross section you just built. And with that your master blacksmith's forge is complete. We'll be sprucing the rest of it up later.

10

HOME IMPROVEMENTS

It's time for some home makeovers. Find the L-shape house if possible (although any house will do). Knock out the walls and replace them with white terracotta. Then with dark oak wood, mine the corners of the house and build spikes in their place.

11

ROOF REBUILDING

Demolish the roof and then build up the walls by five blocks, again with white terracotta. Head back to the dark oak wood and continue the spikes up the sides of the new walls. When that's all done, connect the dark oak horizontally to create a frame effect.

12

A NEW COLOR

We'll be putting the roof back on in a different shade. Grab dark oak planks and run them along the front top of the house and along the back left. Create a step effect going up. The front should be eight blocks high, while the back is six blocks tall.

THE IRON GOLEM

STAIRS INTO A ROOF

With some dark oak wood stairs, extend the front section so it becomes parallel with the beginning of the back section. Extend the back section across the house. Finish by running stairs one block below the roof and add in windows in the center of each section.

YOU DON'T want to make an enemy out of an Iron Golem. These giant statues can spawn in villages if there is a 16x16x16 clear area, centered on the 21 or more houses in the village and if there are at least 10 villagers living there. One Iron Golem has a chance of spawning every six minutes.

BEING 2.7 blocks tall and 1.4 blocks wide, these giants can deliver a devastating blow if you annoy them. They LOVE the villagers, and if you attack a villager, or the Golem, they will come after you! One hit will cause between 7 and 21 damage to your heart meter and send you flying into the air!

THE BEST way of dealing with an Iron Golem is to simply run away! Keep out of their reach for a short time and they will forget about you and calm down. If you want to kill them off though, the most effective methods are lava, fire, cacti, poison, or suffocation—they are hard nuts to crack! You can attack them with regular weapons, but you need to be close.

TRY MAKING a pit—an enclosed area where you can start a fire across the floor. If you can lure an Iron Golem into it, it will only last a minute before popping! Lava is even more effective; they can only last 13 seconds in lava. They don't like the spikes on cacti either. More complicated is suffocation. It can be achieved by making a trap that has pistons placed to squash the Iron Golem; squeezed of breath they will only last around 25 seconds.

SIMILAR, BUT DIFFERENT

Every village has multiple houses, so let's pick another and repeat what we did in the last few steps. This time start with the roof—mine up one block, replace with dark oak, and repeat until it's completed. Dig up the walls and replace them with terracotta.

MIX IT UP

You can always leave this until later, but now is a great time to make over all the remaining houses so they match the previous ones we just showed you how to do. If you prefer a different design, change the walls to a mix of stone bricks and cracked stone bricks.

WRECKING BALL!

It's now time to go back to our blacksmith's forge that we rebuilt earlier on. See that cabin on the right? Wreck it. In its place, build walls on the right and back sides, add in dark oak like we did for our houses, and add a layer of stone half slabs on top.

ADD SOME WINDOWS

Extend the roof and dark oak frame so it goes all the way around the blacksmith's forge area. After you've laid down the half slabs on top, dig out a cross-shaped hole directly above the forge. Lastly, add in windows around the structure—we used glass panes.

A SMOKING CHIMNEY

Head to the cross-shaped hole and with stone bricks, extend the chimney of the forge up into the air by four blocks. Run half slabs around the base of where the chimney pokes out, then with cobwebs create a step effect from the top of the chimney, like smoke!

SMARTEN UP THE INSIDE

Head to the inside, and in the right section, mine the floor and lay down a cobblestone and stone brick pattern to match our village paths. Add a single stone step to act as a chair, and create a cooling pit by laying down a rectangle of half slabs and fill with water.

WELL, WELL, WELL!

Find the village well—they all have one—because we're going to spruce it up. When found, destroy it (and get rid of the water!). Create a stone brick L shape, leaving the front section open by one block. The diameter should be 3x3 blocks when viewed from above.

TAKE YOUR TIME

Get your stone brick stairs once more and run them around the outside of the L shape. This next part is tricky, so take it slowly. Lay stairs on top of the other stairs, only upside down this time. You should be left with a kind of C shape around the L shape.

LOOKING GOOD

With cobblestone wall, build on top of the L shape by two blocks in four sets of pillars, then create a two-block-high cube. On the upper part of the cube, run stairs around the outside and mine up the corners. Place four stairs facing outward, with a half slab in the middle.

23

LEAVES AND BLOCKS...

Like the well, the naturally spawning village farming areas aren't the best, so let's fix that. With leaves and dark oak wood, create the shape in the picture. It's one dark oak wood block followed by two leaves blocks.

24

THE VEGETABLE PATCH

Extend each of the dark oak blocks up by one. On top of the leaves, grab dark oak fence and run it between the wood. Then with a hoe, plant some vegetation of your choosing. Adding some more decorative parts, use stone buttons added to each of the dark oak blocks.

25

CREEPER WATCH

To round out our project, all we need is a decent lookout post. Create a 4x4 stone brick square somewhere overlooking the village. Mine the corners, and replace with dark oak. Next, build the walls really high, so you can see the entire village from the top.

26

KEEP A LOOKOUT

At the very top of your new tower run dark oak half slabs around the outside. On top of the half slabs, add in a ring of dark oak fence too — you don't want to fall off! Next, build the inside corners—the dark oak corners—up by five blocks.

27

THE FINISHING TOUCH

Grab your stairs for the final time and run them on top of the dark oak to create a square. One block in and up one block, add another smaller square made of stairs. Keep doing this until you reach the top. Add torches to the fence and your village makeover is complete!

KING OF THE JUNGLE!

Build your own jungle tree house high up above the ground!

Fancy spending time in a jungle-set home away from home? Sick of the ground and love the thought of hanging out high up in the trees? Well then, you're in the right place! Follow our step-by-step builder's guide and you'll have a fabulous tree house to call your own in just a couple of hours! The following guide is straightforward to follow and produces great results!

1

PLATFORMER

To get your base up high, you'll first need to build some platforms for it to stand on. Build three or four on different trees at various different heights. The tallest will be your main base.

2

CLIMB UP

You'll need a way to reach those platforms, but instead of using stairs, use slabs that wind around the trunks of your trees to reach the platforms—that way it will look more natural.

3

ON THE BRIDGE

Getting up is easy, but jumping between trees is harder. You'll want to use slabs again to make mini bridges, but don't make them straight. Put in some dips as it'll look better.

4

FENCED IN

The problem with trees and heights is that it's really easy to fall off! Add fence posts to your platforms so you're a bit safer—plus, it makes them look more like proper platforms.

INSPIRATION

TREE HOUSE

This simple gem from battlenations looks like a house up a tree!

HOUSE TREE

Kartticrg, on the other hand, gives us a house shaped like a tree!

LUXURY LIFE

Just look at the classy interiors that DiNozzo37 has designed!

5 BRANCH OUT

At your tallest platform you'll want to start adding extra branches to the tree using jungle wood. Have some going down for mini doorways, and some going up so it's almost like a frame.

6 EXTEND BACK

One tree platform is too small for a house, so extend it backward so it reaches a second one, or so it sits on top of a shorter one. Keep it a funny shape instead of making it square.

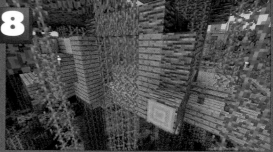

7 WALLED IN

Time to start adding your walls. Make them a mix of jungle planks and wood branches and keep them three-high. It's a tree house, so it's going to feel small! Some areas can be taller, though.

8 VINE VIEW

It looks good if you have lots of different-sized windows, like little ones in branches, and big full wall-sized ones. We dropped vines down in front of this one to make it feel more like a jungle.

9 CUBBY HOLES

You want the whole thing to look natural, so build around any branches instead of moving them, and keep some vines and leaves inside too. Those vines can be used as ladders.

10 EXTRA BALCONY

Add more floors to your build in one small area. Use glass panes to make your balcony look modern, or build downward to make a small hanging basement if it suits your tree better.

11

MESSY IS BEST

Keep working your way around remembering to keep it natural looking. Use slabs for your roof or floor to give it a different shape. Don't forget to put in lots of windows to let the light in!

12

TIDY UP

Now the outside is done, it's time to patch up inside. Add some wood trunks to the floor in random spots to look like branches coming up. Add leaves to keep it looking like you're in a tree.

13

OPEN PLAN

Now it's decorating time! Use stairs to make a comfy sofa near your biggest window, and make your smallest corner a cozy bedroom. A dining table in the middle ties it all together.

INSPIRATION

MULTISTORY

We think we'd like to live in ShinyBlock's many-tiered build in real life!

COUNTRY SPREAD

TheKingRuizz has built a fantastic tree house as big as a village!

SKY FARM

iOBu has gone all in and crafted some tree-bound farms, too!

14

GO NATURAL

Step back and admire your work! To make it look even more like a tree house, switch on the natural texture pack on consoles, or try the fantasy one. It makes the leaves extra bushy looking.

SIMPLE TRICKS

This is a really easy design if you've got windows that are one block wide. Use a trapdoor over the top, leave a gap, and then place any block. Then put a gate on top of that, destroy the block, open the gate, and you're done!

Use my expert building tips!

WINDOW SHOPPING!

Spruce up your builds with these window designs!

SHUTTER UP

This works on any window shape, not just narrow ones. Place ladders on either side of a window to make it look like shutters.

STONE COVER

The cover here is made of cobblestone stairs and slabs, then cobblestone fence underneath that turns into wooden fence posts.

These won't help in the nether!

ARCHES

Go one step further by adding shutters made of ladders, a ledge made of slabs, and an archway over the top also made of slabs.

CUT IN

Want to make it look like your windows are farther back into your wall? Than use stairs on the top and bottom. Glass panes line up just right with the thin part of the step.

SMALL BOOTH

This is a great rustic look. Instead of ladders use trapdoors for shutters. It uses lots of stair blocks again but in different patterns. They're so handy for making lots of different shapes!

GLASS FREE

This design is great for desert builds. You don't always need to use glass for windows. These two designs use stairs and slabs to make a pattern. You could make any pattern you like!

Build me a coop with a view!

Let's build it!

A FLYING HOUSE

Taking off into the sky – just like in the movie *Up*!

INFO

FLYING HOUSE

Difficulty:
HARD

There is some tricky detail in this build, but you can do it!

Time needed:
1¾ HOURS

START HERE

1 **GRAB SOME** stone bricks, spruce wood, and a door and build the shape shown in the picture above to act as your guideline for the house. Start with a row of five. On the right, drop eight. Turn, then seven. Turn again, then five. And finally, snake the wall back around onto itself.

2 **BUILD ALL** the walls up by five blocks and add a door in the gap. Above the door frame area, create a step effect. Here's a bonus tip: The Skyrim mash-up pack has some great textures for medieval buildings, but other blocks, like wool, aren't the best to work with.

3 **ARM YOURSELF** with some spruce wood steps. From the step effect, run steps along the side of the larger section of the house. Continue this up one level until you have the entire larger section covered. Then, move onto the right section and do the same.

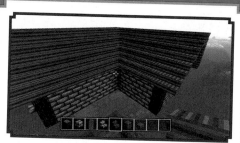

4 **IN THE** space in between the two sections, lay a stone brick floor. For the lamppost, lay four spruce wood blocks and surround the base with steps. At the top add glowstone. Below and above the glowstone, run steps. Fill the gaps with fencing, and run half slabs around the middle.

5 GRAB SOME white terracotta blocks and then build a flat circle that has a main length seven blocks long. On the back side, build everything out by seven blocks to create a sphere shape, a bit like a football or globe.

6 HEAD TO each of the flat, square shapes and knock out the corners. Then, in the natural gaps that have formed, connect the square shapes around to each other so you're left with four jagged spikes. On top and below, create a pyramid formation to form the balloon.

7 YOU NOW have two options for how to finish: Step 7 on its own, or Step 8 and Step 9. For the hot-air balloon, pull out red terracotta and build a shell around the upper half of the balloon. Build fencing with sea lanterns coming off the longer parts, then create a pattern on the shell from wool.

8 OR YOU can build a bunch of balloons instead. Here's how we did it: Head to the base of the sphere and with white terracotta, create flat squares one block smaller than the last, then knock the corners out of each of them. Lastly, run fencing down to the house.

BUILD THIS!

Let's see how many of those balloons I can pop with my arrows!

9 NOW TO finish, head into the second page of the Creative menu and press Down until you find the wool sections. Fill your hotbar with different colored wools, then cover the entire sphere in all of those different wools. Don't put two colors together or they will stand out from a distance. Well done—you've made lots of balloons!

MINECRAFT CRIBS

We all want a cool pad to retreat to after a hard day's crafting. So here's some ace homemaking tips . . .

Welcome to Minecraft Cribs, with me, your host, Nice Cube. Today we're gonna be looking at the classiest, biggest, weirdest, and craziest Minecraft creations, from the easily doable to the absolutely insane.

Basic shelters with beds, torches, and chests are for your Minecraft noobs and people with low standards—you want some fitting tribute to your Minecraft skills, and these cribs are the best way to show everyone who's the boss of the blocks.

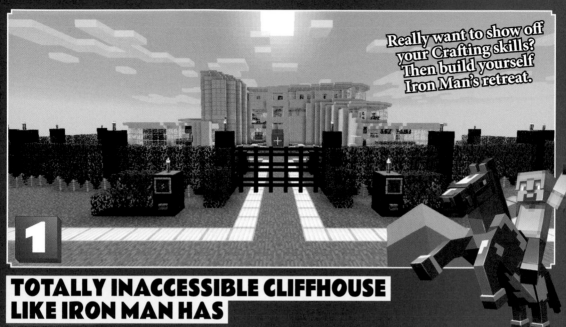

Really want to show off your Crafting skills? Then build yourself Iron Man's retreat.

1

TOTALLY INACCESSIBLE CLIFFHOUSE LIKE IRON MAN HAS

So, Notch probably has the best house in all the world, having a mansion that cost roughly a bazillion dollars and has its own M&M room. Maybe all the toilets can talk, and the swimming pool is so deep it's heated by the earth's core. Who knows. We'll never get to see it. But one thing Notch doesn't have—that he can never have—is a replica of Tony Stark's house in *Iron Man*. (Disclaimer: Notch could totally have this, too, but he's busy discussing politics with his toilet). All you have to do is create a beautiful, cliff-top house with views across the vista, complete with spiral staircase, sarcastic robot butler, and secret underground superhero lab. Honestly, it's not that difficult. You can even add your very own candy room, if you wish. Just try not to annoy any super-powerful arms dealers, yeah?

2

Get away from it all and float around in the sky!

CLOUD HOUSE IN THE SKY

Now if you're feeling a bit superior you'll be reading all of these suggestions and thinking that none of them could possibly live up to how incredibly awesome and better than everyone else you are. You don't want to have to share the earth with these simple humans, do you? Of course not. The only way to avoid all that is to go big or go home—or, in this case, both—because your home is IN THE SKY. Combine the perks of having a nearly inaccessible home with the joys of never having to see another being by hiding your house inside a great big cloud. No one will even know you're up there. Of course, the building period might give it away, as you'll have to build a bridge or a tower to get up there with all your materials . . . but there are ways to deal with anyone who sees you. Muhahahaha . . .

Make yourself a cozy home in the fiery wastes of the Nether.

3

NETHER

You're a risk taker. You're the kind of person who stares danger right in the face. There's only one kind of house for you: a house in hell. Minecraft has the Nether—a dark, lava-filled place teeming with horrible mobs, and a ton of rare materials. But if you want to build yourself a hellbase, you'll need to come prepared: Build it around your portal so you can escape at any time, make sure to keep away from lava and netherrack, and be sure to build your floor out of transparent blocks to prevent mob spawning. You can build your home out of anything non-burnable—cobblestone is probably easiest, but obsidian looks cooler—and you can mine it in the Nether (if you're careful). Of course, you'll have to make sure not to disturb the zombie pigmen if you take this route. Enjoy your new life in hell!

Every day can be Christmas with this festive homestead!

4

FESTIVE CHRISTMAS HOUSE FROM HELL

Ohhh, I wish it could be Christmas every day! Excellent news: It can be when your house looks like something Santa threw up. There's plenty of red and green in the standard Minecraft texture pack, although you can download a mod or check out the pack that comes with the console versions. Why not build a skyscraper that looks like a candy cane, the stable from the nativity, or just a big old festive mansion? Start with some red clay and white quartz if you want to keep it classy, and add in green. Make sure to have a nice brick fireplace inside, and, of course, a Christmas tree. Use something like a pyramid of bushes with a little yellow flower on top, and random colored blocks underneath as presents. If you want a perfect example of a Christmas house, use cobwebs as snowflakes.

Building the perfect siege-proof home has one big problem - how do YOU get in?

5

THE ULTIMATE SIEGE-PROOF HOME

No matter how beautiful, time-consuming, or well-hidden your Minecraft creations are, there's always some roaming mob, or even worse, other players ready to mess up your hard work. So you have to make sure you attack-proof your house. Then why not create the ultimate in siege-proof dwellings. Lava moats, explosion-proof obsidian walls, a fence to stop spiders on both the ground and the roof, plenty of lighting to stop mob spawns, and as many pressure plates and redstone-powered contraptions as you can figure out.

But how do YOU get inside such a fortress? However you get in might also end up being the way a smart invader gets in, after all. So you'll have to be extra smart to outsmart the smart: hide a pressure plate somewhere that triggers a wall to open. Chances of theft: minimal.

No one's going to risk going through that lava cascade to post you junk mail!

6

HIDDEN LAVA WATERFALL CAVE

Sometimes you don't want to be bothered. Sometimes, you really, really don't want to be bothered. The former gets a menacing dog; the latter builds their house behind a lava waterfall. If you want to know how to keep unwanted guests away, get one of these—but be warned, nature is as much your enemy as anyone on the other side of the lava waterfall. You'll probably want a secret, well-hidden entrance that you can use to get into the lava house—maybe build a staircase under a tree, or, if you're a bit of a Minecraft whiz, make yourself a proper hidden door with a few automated pistons. The only problem with a house hidden behind a waterfall is that you might become a James Bond villain. If that's a risk you're prepared to take, embrace it and build yourself a huge aquarium wall . . .

PLAYING MINECRAFT IN 3-D

Switch on 3-D in your game, grab a pair of 3-D glasses, and let's play Minecraft in three dimensions!

Video Settings

Graphics: Fancy

Smooth Lighting: Maximum

3D Anaglyph: ON

GUI Scale: Large

Brightness: Bright

Particles: All

Use VSync: ON

Use VBOs: ON

Render Distance: 18 chunks

Max Framerate: Unlimited

View Bobbing: ON

Attack Indicator: Crosshair

Clouds: OFF

Fullscreen: OFF

Mipmap Levels: 4

Entity Shadows: ON

Done

TIP 1

SWITCH IT ON!

Have you ever seen that option, hidden away in the "Video Settings" menu of Minecraft? 3-D Anaglyph: OFF or ON! It makes the screen go very strange with red-and-blue shadows all over it. Well, there's a reason for that. An "anaglyph" is a type of 3-D photograph that has been around since 1853. That's 164 years! And your game of Minecraft has a hidden 3-D option inside it!

TIP 2

IT'S A TRICK!

For as long as there has been photography, people have experimented with 3-D pictures for one simple reason: Our eyes are set slightly apart, and this is what makes what you see feel real. Close one eye and you will see what we mean. Your world will change to 2-D and everything will feel flat. Open both eyes and you get a feeling of depth in everything around you. This is what 3-D Anaglyph images try to trick your brain to see!

The 3-D glasses you get in modern movies won't work, it's only the red-and-blue style of 3-D that works with Minecraft.

TIP 3

YOU'LL NEED SOME GLASSES!

These are essential for 3-D! Unfotunately, you can't use the ones you get at the movies, but it's easy to make your own! First, create a glasses shape from thick cardboard. (If you have an old pair of glasses lying around you could use these instead!). Glue some clear plastic where the lenses are and then color one lens red and one lens blue—and you're done! Make sure to ask a parent before cutting anything out!

Try the 3-D effect in Minecraft for just a few minutes at first as it gives some people a headache. If you're fine, you can try again!

TIP 4

THE WORLD IN 3-D!

Now try moving around. The experts at Mojang created Minecraft with 3-D Anaglyph visuals in mind, so every block, every object, every mob— even the clouds—all change their 3-D appearance depending on where you are standing in the world. The effect has been tried in 2-D and it was big for a while in movies, but to have a 3-D game generating these images in real time is great!

TIP 5

COLOR IT IN!

Once your mask's pixels are colored in, you're good to go. Now go to the "3-D Anaglyph" option in the "Visual Settings" and select ON. Jump into the game in your favorite saved world and rather than seeing Minecraft in the usual 2-D style, everything will have red-and-blue shadows. The way it works is the bigger the shadows cast by objects, the closer or farther away they seem to you in 3-D!

THE ULTIMATE BUILDER'S MANUAL

Take your builds to the next level with these expert tips!

Ever wanted to make your builds look like all the pros you see online? Then we've got some great tips and secrets that will turn your basic huts into fantastic-looking houses. These hints are super easy to try but make a huge difference. You'll be a pro Minecraft builder in no time!

1

ADD FRAMES TO ALL YOUR HOUSES

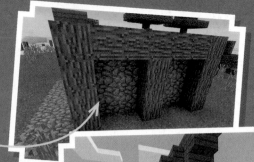

A basic hut will keep you safe for your first few nights, but it's not very exciting to look at! Neither is just making an even bigger square building. A really easy way to improve a build is to add a frame made of any kind of wood all the way around it. From there you can add a roof with a second floor. It works on both small and big builds.

2

EXPERIMENT WITH ROOF TYPES

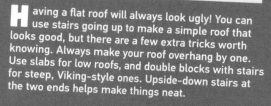

H aving a flat roof will always look ugly! You can use stairs going up to make a simple roof that looks good, but there are a few extra tricks worth knowing. Always make your roof overhang by one. Use slabs for low roofs, and double blocks with stairs for steep, Viking-style ones. Upside-down stairs at the two ends helps make things neat.

3

DON'T FORGET GARDENS

The area outside your build is just as important as the actual building. Creating an area outside the front that keeps with the theme ties it all together. Think plain lawns and bushes for cities, and fields of flowers for country cottages.

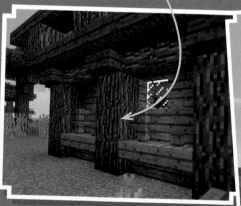

 # 4 TURN UPSIDE DOWN

One of the easiest, best tricks of all is turning stairs upside down to make all sorts of things. They're great for adding texture to walls, and making the underside of roofs nice and neat. Add them under windows to make ledges, and you can even use them for decking too.

JUST ADD WATER

Does your build look a little flat? Then incorporate water features! Water is everywhere in real life so it makes sense to include it in your builds. For example, fountains are great in plazas, ponds are great for relaxing by, and rivers are great for building bridges over. Every desert town needs a well, too.

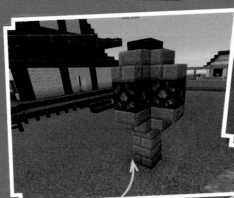

MORE THAN TORCHES

Getting enough light for towns is always a problem, and the normal torches can get a bit boring after a while. Mix it up by using redstone to make lights that turn on automatically at night, lanterns made of glowstone and trap doors that hang down, or flaming torches made with netherack.

7

PLOT PATHS

Linking your buildings together with paths will really make it feel like a city or town, but you need to think carefully about paths. Wooded areas will only need a rugged dirt path made from different block types. Sand or gravel paths are good for contrast. If you're in a city, use stairs with slabs to give paths a border, or use full blocks to make it look like gutters.

8

WALL YOURSELF IN STYLE

Another way to easily boost your builds is by adding detail to all of your walls. There's nothing worse than a flat wall—just adding beams can make a huge difference, or adding an extra layer so you can make a pattern with stair blocks. Adding arches made of slabs to windows and doors adds loads of depth.

9
REMEMBER THE MAGIC NUMBERS

This is a weird tip, but a really important one! Being aware of numbers helps you plan your builds so much better—if you only build in odd numbers, like five or 11 then your roof will always line up in the middle. Make big walls three thick so you can add in details. If you plan an area, think in 15x15 chunks and put them together. It's a great size for a full, tall apartment building, or a country house with a garden. It'll also help break down any really big builds. Think of it like land plots all coming together!

10
PICK MATCHING COLORS

A big cobblestone city in a desert can look really out of place, so make all of your buildings match the local area by using the materials from that biome. For example, sandstone if you're in a desert, and acacia wood houses if you're in the savanna. You can use other materials, but use them for fancy details only rather than the main buildings so it's not the main focus.

ESSENTIAL ITEMS

The things that every Minecraft legend needs in their inventory . . .

There are plenty of challenges to face in Minecraft, from fighting tricky enemies, to mining rare resources, to completing your own ambitious building projects. To meet all of these challenges, you'll need some important items in your inventory. Here we pick out the ones that you just can't go without—from early-game basics, to powerful late-game items.

BED

The humble bed is an overlooked item. When you're exploring deep, dangerous mines looking for rare materials, you should always have a bed handy to set a spawn point close by. This will make it easy to recover any lost items if you run into trouble on your journey.

ENCHANTED GOLDEN APPLE

Crafted with blocks of gold and an apple, the enchanted golden apple will temporarily give you eight hearts of absorption health and will regenerate your health over a short period of time. This makes it an essential item to take into battle against tough mobs.

DIAMONDS

Want to craft the best stuff in Minecraft? Then you're going to need diamonds. Diamond armor to protect you from mob attacks, diamond swords to deal heavy damage, diamond axes, diamond shovels, and so on. Diamonds are also needed to craft an enchanting table.

MINECART

Whatever your goal in Minecraft, you're going to need resources to do it. Building yourself a track and putting a minecart on it to help transport materials from deep mines, back to the smelters and crafting table at your base of operation, is a great way of getting things done.

ENCHANTED BOOK

With a book and an enchanting table, you can create an enchanted book. These can then be used to apply special effects to your weapons, tools, and armor. You can increase their damage, improve mining speed, increase your luck when fishing, and walk on water!

PICKAXE

Where would we be without the humble pickaxe? Gold, iron, stone, coal, diamonds, and the many other resources you collect come from swinging this vital tool. It may well be the most important thing in the whole of Minecraft.

THE 10 BEST PETS IN MINECRAFT

Ordinary, exotic, or extremely dangerous — why not try taming these 10 incredible Minecraft pets!

Now it can be a lonely existence playing this Minecraft thing. Whether you're building a glorious palace for yourself, or just having a fun adventure, it's always nicer to have other people with you. But when your friends aren't around you don't have to ditch the pickaxe — get yourself a pet and you'll never be alone again! You can share your adventures with Tweety, Fluffy, or Mr. Wuffles, or you can just keep them at home. The thing is, there's a limited amount of beasts you can keep as pets, but we're choosing to bend the definition a bit and accept that all captured animals count. Yay, variety!

PIG

The humble pig is one of the easier animals to tame and domesticate in Minecraft, making him a great choice for the beginner who wants a little bit of oinky company. First, lure your potential porky pal into an enclosed area with some carrots—this is where you'll be keeping him, so you can stick to the basics and build a little fenced-off pen. Or you could go dramatic and build him a tiny pig house. Once he's in his new home, close it off so he can't escape, and voilà! Your very own piggy pal!

CHICKEN

So now you have your own pigs, you're looking to expand, right? Time to start turning your livestock collection into a farm with chickens. As with pigs, lure them into an enclosed area (but this time using wheat seeds), then block them in. Chickens give you eggs every five to ten minutes. Killing them gives you raw chicken, and killing them with fire gives you cooked chicken. Now we've got bacon and eggs sorted!

MOOSHROOM

You've got yourself some pigs and chickens, and you're well on your way to starting a pretty decent farm. What else do farms need? Cows, probably. But you're bored of your garden-variety domesticated farmyard animals, so it's time to get a little more exciting. A mooshroom is a sort of cross between a regular cow and a mushroom, and the less you know about why that happened the better. They're dappled red and white, with huge fungi all over their backs. Like regular cows they can be milked with a bucket, or killed to create leather and beef. However, shearing them will give you red mushrooms. Yum!

OCELOT

Wolves may be the dogs of the Minecraft world, but ocelots are the cats. In the wild, they appear as yellow-and-black-spotted cats, stalking chickens and scaring away creepers. They won't attack you, but they can sprint—so you'll have to be clever if you want to catch one. With an uncooked fish, wait for one to approach, then stay VERY still. They should follow you home and become your best friend.

SILVERFISH

The best thing about having silverfish as pets is that they're so tiny you can have loads, and they take up hardly any space. The first thing to remember is that they aren't actual fish, so don't make the mistake of building them a big watery tank only to find them drowned in the morning. You may recognize them from strongholds, where smashing a block that looks suspiciously like all the other stone blocks will spawn a wiggly, little dude intent on destroying you. The best plan is to create a nice cage for them first. In creative mode, place a silverfish spawn block inside where you want them to be, and destroy it. They're the Minecraft equivalent of sea monkeys! Watch them wiggle!

WOLF

They might be fairly rare, and you might have to venture deep into the dark woods or the chilly tundra to find them, but a tamed wolf is the closest thing to man's best friend in Minecraft. Grab yourself a few bones to tame a wild wolf—each has a one in three chance of taming the little guy, so keep trying if it doesn't work the first time around. Once you've succeeded, then your new friend will get a nice orange collar, and will sit down before following you around.

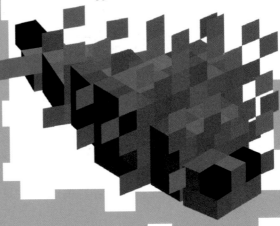

HORSE

You'll find horses roaming the plains alongside donkeys, in 35 different colors. You can get brown, dark brown, even darker brown, black, gray, white, plus all of the above with various types of spots—whereas donkeys just come in your boring standard gray-brown. Sorry, donkeys. Unfortunately, horses are a bit trickier to tame than the animals we've seen so far, requiring you to mount them over and over again until the horse no longer bucks you off. Feeding them sugar and wheat will increase your chances, and a golden apple will also make a horse enter breeding mode. It's hard work, but you can put armor on horses, making them the coolest pet you can own.

ELDER GUARDIAN

Now if farmyard animals bore you, then maybe you're ready for the ultimate challenge – turning the elder guardian into your personal plaything. It looks like a cross between a really gross fish and a sea mine, and the secret to capturing this tricky beast is patience. You'll need to be invisible so it doesn't kill you, and you'll need loads of minecart tracks to push him toward his new prison. Also get milk, as your new pet has a habit of giving you mining fatigue.

SPIDER

Nothing is more cuddly than an adorable spider, crawling all over your hands and face and into your mouth. No? Not a fan of spiders? Perhaps you'll still enjoy having them as pets, merely because a spider in a cage is a spider that's not in your mouth. You'll find them scuttling about anywhere that's dark, like caves, but darkness also makes them hostile, so be careful. Make sure it's nighttime, and lure the spider back to the little home. Once you've trapped him, make sure to close off the ceiling so he can't climb out . . .

ZOMBIE PIGMAN

Now we're getting really interesting. Who said all your pets had to be animals? Technically, the zombie pigman isn't really human or animal – he's a pigman, which makes him a bit of both, and therefore it's totally acceptable to keep him/it as a pet. Because Minecraft doesn't encourage the capture and keeping of monsters as pets, there's no real way to lure him. You'll just have to make him pursue you to his new prison/home.

INFO

THE GREAT FIRE OF 1666
Difficulty:
HARD
Time needed:
10+ HOURS
EXTRA INFO:
Three downloadable maps from the Museum of London

THE GREAT FIRE OF LONDON!

3 hot maps from the Museum of London to download and spray with water!

MUSEUM OF LONDON

GREAT FIRE 1666
EXPERIENCE THE STORY IN MINECRAFT

Fire! FIRE! It's 1666 and the city of London is on fire. It all started in a bakery in Pudding Lane when some smoldering embers caught alight and set the wooden building on fire, quickly spreading next door. Around the bakery there were barrels of tar and brandy, which helped the flames take hold!

Who said history was boring, eh? The experts at the Museum of London got together with a team of Minecraft techs to create not one, not two, but three hot (oh yes, they're hot!) maps of London 351 years ago — and we've got top tips

on playing all three. There's something here for all skill levels.

● Map 1 is called Pre-Fire and teaches you what happened back in 1666.

● Map 2 is called The Fire and has you running around putting out the fire.

● Map 3 is called The Rebuild and gives you the chance to rebuild the city yourself.

Download the maps from . . .
museumoflondon.org.uk/discover/ great-fire-1666

1 PRE-FIRE

IT'S 1666

You start in a boat on the River Thames and must find your way off. There's a ladder you can climb, explore around the boat until you find it. The objective is to find 12 audio records to discover what caused the Great Fire. Keep your eyes open for maps.

2

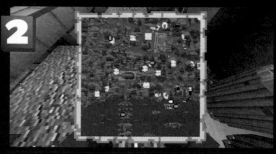

KNOW YOUR MAPS

As you explore, when you pick up maps you will see that special areas are marked in green. Your location is in white. You will also spot landmarks like London Bridge, the Thames, and St. Paul's Cathedral. Find a secret, and you'll get an audio clip of London's history!

3

HEY, IT'S STAMPY!

You learn as you play in this map. Did you know there were other fires before the Great one? One made London Bridge fall down! You might recognize one of the voices in the audio records you find—it's none other than Stampylongnose himself!

4

SPEEDING UP

The maps of London are huge! Don't be afraid to use the "Sprint" key to speed up your exploration of the streets. One of the most impressive buildings is St. Paul's Cathedral. Walk around the outside until you find a ladder to climb leading up the side.

5

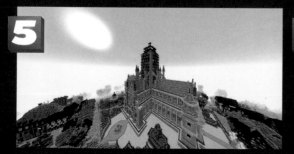

CLIMB A CATHEDRAL

The ladders lead up the side of the building and over the roof and will lead to another audio record telling of a fire that damaged the cathedral. You will find a sketch of the cathedral as you go along. The fire started in a baker's shop in Pudding Lane.

6

OFF WITH HER HEAD!

Head right from London Bridge, and you will find your way to the Tower of London. There are some amazing sailing ships down on the water. See if you can find the Traitor's Gate that leads from the water into the tower. This is where traitors were brought to meet their fate!

1 THE FIRE

2

DAY ONE GAME

When you start Map 2 you will find yourself inside a museum. There are exhibits around you that will teach you about fire hooks, water squirts, leather buckets, and all the things you will need to help fight the fire. Then you can start the day-one game.

CAN YOU SMELL BURNING?

You're in bed, the flames are licking around you, and you've got to get moving to save yourself, your house, and London! Touch any flame and you'll be set on fire, so you'd better put some of it out! No, don't pull the duvet up and go back to sleep!

3

4

GRAB AN AX!

The trick is to use an ax to smash the windows in the top floor of your house. You'll then be able to find the back stairs that will lead out to the street. Now get to Pudding Lane. (You can teleport if you find the sign.) Some people have tips, so be sure to stop to chat.

FIND THE CHURCH

Fire-fighting equipment is kept in the church in the center of the map, so make your way there. You will pass other large buildings that look like churches, but don't be confused. The church you want has large clear glass windows and a large entrance way.

5

6

FIRE-FIGHTING GEAR

Inside the church, you will find a water squirt. Grab this, then you need a source of water to make the squirt work. Try troughs, puddles, the river. Hopefully, by exploring London in Map 1 you will have already gotten an idea of the best places to look for water.

WHERE'S THE WATER?

Fill leather buckets with water to keep your squirt topped up. While you are searching, the fire will be spreading. The fire hook can be used to stop it. You will see the connecting blocks high above the street—use the hook to pull them down and stop the fire.

1 THE REBUILD

LONG LIVE THE KING!

Now it's time to rebuild our capital city. The Museum of London has just launched the third map in their trilogy of Great Fire Minecraft maps. It's called "The Rebuild." Start by exploring the ruined streets, then you will discover King Charles II at the Guildhall.

2

FOUR HEADS ARE BETTER THAN ONE

The map has four architects (they're the people who design buildings) for you to interact with: Christopher Wren, Valentine Knight, John Evelyn, and Richard Newport. Each of these men had their own unique ideas of how London could be rebuilt.

3

52 CHURCHES!

Christopher Wren actually built 52 churches around London after the Great Fire. It was the equivalent of Minecraft, only 351 years ago, and using a lot larger blocks! After listening to the four architects, you can decide how you would like to rebuild your version.

TOOLS OF THE TRADE

WATER SQUIRT You can find these in churches—that's where they kept them back in 1666. You will need a source of water for them to work.

FIRE HOOK Fire can spread from one building to another quickly, you can stop this by pulling down timbers between buildings with a fire hook.

LEATHER BUCKET These can carry enough water to put out a few flames, but you will need to learn where the puddles and river are to keep topped up!

4

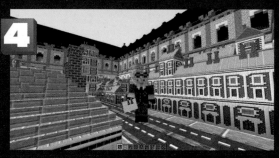

STAR VOICES

You will get to talk with lots of characters around "The Rebuild" Minecraft map with voices provided by BigBStaz, NinjaBob, Wizard Keen, and even Stampy's dad playing King Charles II! The Museum of London and their Minecraft team have done an excellent job!

TIPS

This works on...

☒ Computer Edition

☒ Pocket Edition

🎮 Console Edition

SKINS

Steve and Alex are great, but personalizing your skin is the first thing you should do to customize your game. On computers, you upload a new skin file to your Minecraft.net profile page. On console, you can choose from 16 default skins, or buy a skin pack. On Pocket Edition, skin packs can also be bought as in-app purchases.

There are thousands of skins to download – it's Robbie Rotten!

We love this tazmanian devil skin - they've used the body to make his mouth look extra big!

Still playing vanilla Minecraft? There's so much more you can do!

CUSTOMIZING MINECRAFT

The Team Mayhem guide to making the game your own!

This works on...

☒ Computer Edition

MODS

Taking Minecraft to the next level are mods. These files change the game in big ways. There are too many to list, but the ones we like the best are those that add cool content—Mo' Creatures adds in 79 new animals to the game which is a lot of fun. You can find it at mocreatures.org. Galacticraft adds space stuff to the inventory—place a rocket on a launch pad and you can travel to planets all over the galaxy. It's epic! These two need an installer program called Forge installed first. This handles all the tricky placing of files for you. Instructions can be found at files.minecraftforge.net.

Robbie, holding a rocket, surrounded by komodo dragons.

In Galacticraft, you can build rockets, then fly off to distant planets!

RESOURCE PACKS

This works on...

- ▦ Computer Edition
- ▣ Pocket Edition
- 🎮 Console Edition

When textures, 3-D models, music, sound effects, and fonts are all customized together, it's called a Resource Pack. Have you seen those Minecraft pictures with super-realistic water and clouds? That's a Resource Pack in action. On Console Minecraft they call them Mash-Up packs. Some of the best we've seen are the Super Mario Edition on Wii-U, downloadable from the Nintendo eShop, and the new Adventure Time mash-up for all consoles.

RESOURCES

A GOOD place to start is Minecraft.net. It's the central place for everything Minecraft, especially the new Pocket and Windows 10 Add-Ons. We also love planetminecraft.com. A great website run by the Minecraft community packed with skins, texture packs, and mods.

This add-on is called "Alien Invasion". It was used by Mojang to demo add-ons at E3

ADD-ONS

This works on...

- ▣ Pocket Edition

3-D models, textures, and behaviors of mobs can be played with the new add-ons that Mojang is currently trialing on Pocket and Windows 10 Edition. Want a creeper that is the height of a house? You got it! Want pigs that explode on touch? Well, why not? When you've made something really cool, you can then share it with your friends on Minecraft Realms too.

CAPES

This works on...

- ▦ Computer Edition
- 🎮 Console Edition

You've got to be really special to earn yourself a cape in Minecraft! Just like a superhero, it's a special extra item of clothing that not everyone can have. All Mojang staff have special capes with the company logo on them, and players lucky enough to attend the MineCon events could download capes too on both the Computer and Xbox Editions. If you just want to wear a Cape for fun, you can use a mod like the one at MinecraftCapes.co.uk that will allow you to customize your own!

Let's build it!

A SEA MONSTER

A saltwater Halloween fright for you all . . . aarrrgh!

INFO

SEA MONSTER

Difficulty:
NORMAL

There's some tricky detail in this build, but you can do it!

Time needed:
40 MINS

START HERE

1 **FIRST ADD** blue wool, white wool, red wool, and nether wart block to your hotbar. Create a forked tongue out of nether wart—each of the main lengths behind the front of the tongue are three, three, four, and four. From here, create a step structure from blue wool and add in the white and red as shown.

2 **AS A** quick guideline, blue wool is the monster's skin, white are the teeth, and red is used for the mouth. Got it? Cool. Let's move on. Head around to the other side of the tongue and mirror what we just made before filling in the lower blue wool sections.

3 **NOW WE'LL** get to work on the monster's mouth. At the top back of what will be the lower jaw, place one red wool diagonally, then a row of two diagonally from that. On the underside of the last section of the tongue, go one block down and extend the red wool out.

4 **ADD TWO** long diagonal rows at the back, and on the two rows from Step 3, turn the two into a square of four, then drop a block behind each side. Build a five-high frame at the back, extend it out so it's two blocks in depth, fill in the back, and finish with three diagonal rows heading forward.

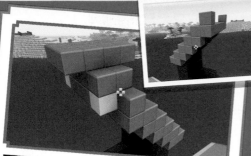

5 **BACK TO** adding in some skin. Pull out your blue wool once more and run a zigzag (Tetris block!) formation along the side of the red wool. Add two blocks on both sides of the top. In between those blocks, build a platform coming off, with two more teeth, and a smaller platform on top.

6 **BY NOW** your monster should be starting to take shape, so let's begin work on the rest of the head. Go back down to the back middle of the jaw. From here, build the skin area away from the zigzags. You should be able to connect this section down so it feeds into the lower jaw.

7 **NEXT COMES** the head and eyes. For this, grab black wool and an eye color (we used lime wool). But before you lay down the eyes, use blue wool to build the front section by the teeth down the middle of the head. On the last section, that's where you can add in the eyes.

8 **THIS NEXT** one is nice and simple. At the back of the head, create an oval shape. The dimensions for this are four on the left and right sides, four single blocks heading inward above and below, then two three-long rows at the top and bottom to connect it all together.

9 **NOW COMES** the last part of the head. From the two 3-long rows, add more rows one block away so it connects into the head. Do this again on the bottom as well. You should be left with a few gaps on either side so go ahead and patch them up with more blue wool.

10 FOR THE first section of the body, go back to the oval shape. Make a mental note of the dimensions from Step 8, then begin building the shape out so it's 10 blocks in length. You can make it longer if you want a bigger sea monster, but for now, stick with 10.

△ Inventory ☐ Creative

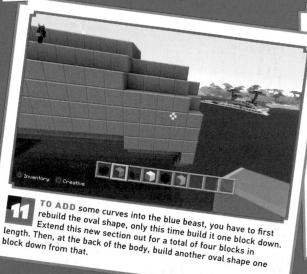

11 TO ADD some curves into the blue beast, you have to first rebuild the oval shape, only this time build it one block down. Extend this new section out for a total of four blocks in length. Then, at the back of the body, build another oval shape one block down from that.

12 AS YOU can see from the image above, the goal now is to build the body out until you reach the water below. For this, just keep creating oval shapes, extending them, and moving each section down by one block. When you're a few blocks underwater, stop building.

13 THE WATER masks the underside of our monster, meaning you don't need to build anything underwater. Neat, eh? Next up, head to the right of Big Blue, and start building an oval from underwater. Continue this up, then when it's high enough, build it back down to water level.

14 FOR THE tail, just build another oval coming out of the water like in the last step, only when you get to the point where the oval isn't submerged, build a flat section coming from the upper half. From here, you should be able to connect the bottom upward toward the flat part.

15 FEEL FREE to go ahead and make Ol' Bitey's teeth much larger (and sharper!). For our last section of this sea monster build, make a three-wide small wing on the left side out of blue wool and light blue wool. Do the same on the opposite side and that's this build complete!

BUILD THIS!

TAKE A RIGHT

This works any time you go underground, but is extra handy when you find a mineshaft. ALWAYS put your torches on the right, that way you can use them as a guide on your way out.

Put them on the right, not left. Right, got it?

MASTER ABANDONED MINESHAFTS!

Never get lost underground again with help from Team Mayhem . . .

CHOP WOOD

Mineshafts often twist around a lot, so if you remove all of the wood, fence, and rails as you go, you'll be able to see where you've explored already.

BRING SHEARS

You'll often find cave spider spawners in mineshafts, so it's a good idea to bring shears with you so you can harvest all those cobwebs for traps! Using a normal sword only gets you string.

MASTER ABANDONED MINESHAFTS!

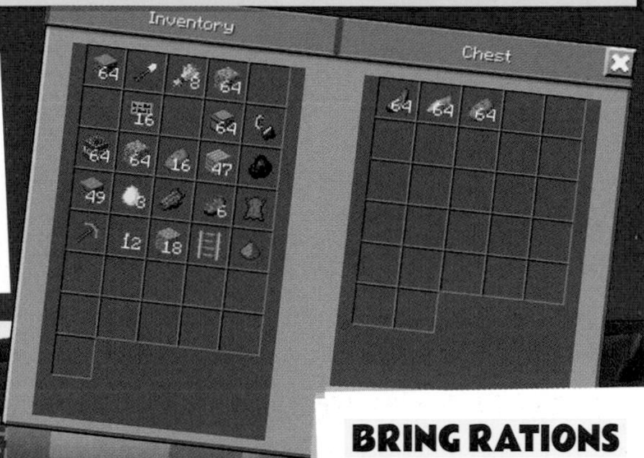
Inventory
Chest

FIND RAVINES AND OCEANS

Mineshafts can be really hard to find. You could easily dig straight past one and never know! But if you look down in oceans and ravines, you'll spot them more easily as you'll be able to see a slight glow where the biome has cut them off.

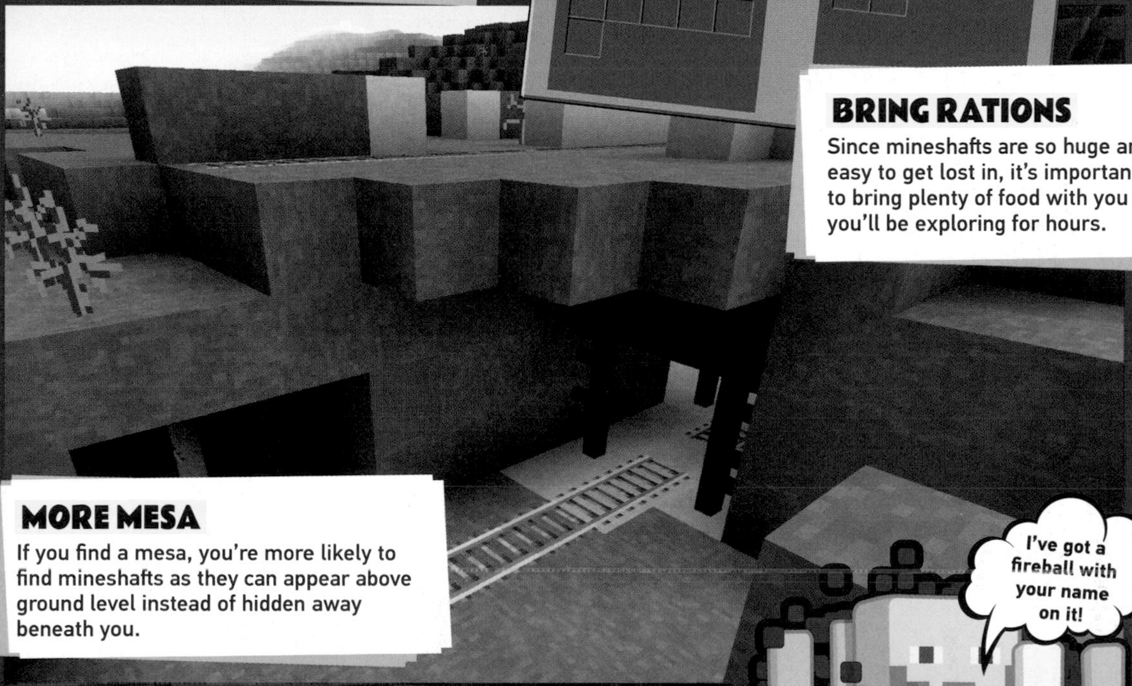

BRING RATIONS

Since mineshafts are so huge and easy to get lost in, it's important to bring plenty of food with you as you'll be exploring for hours.

MORE MESA

If you find a mesa, you're more likely to find mineshafts as they can appear above ground level instead of hidden away beneath you.

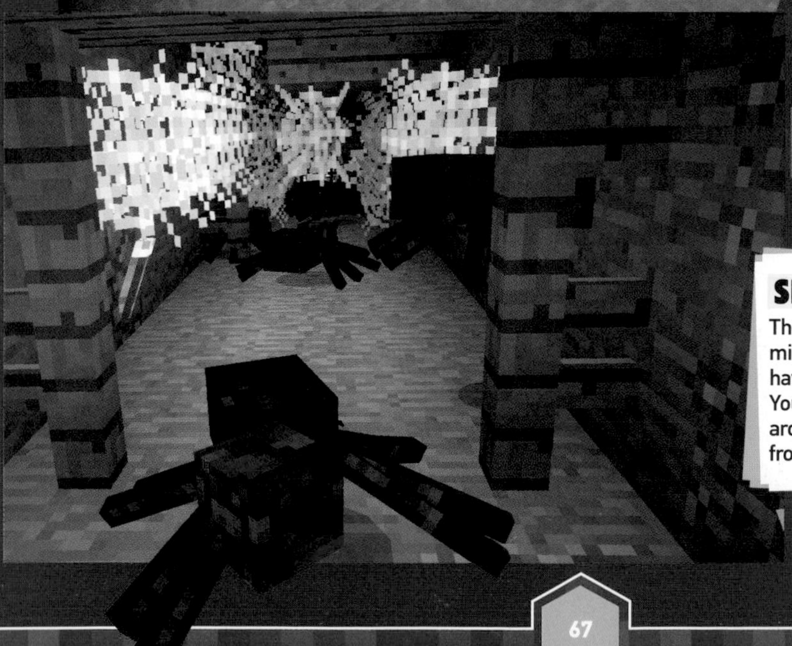

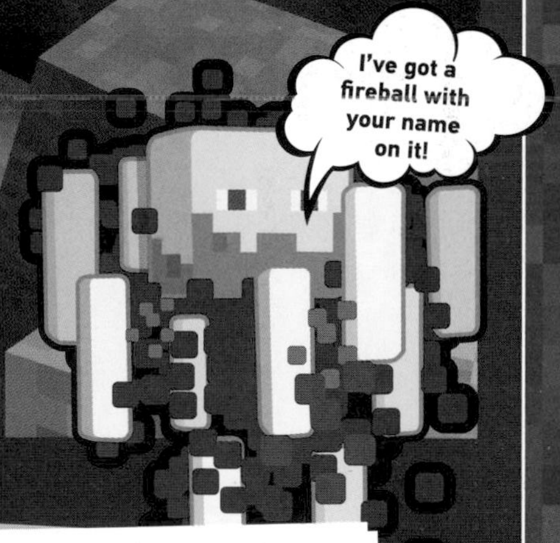
I've got a fireball with your name on it!

SPAWNERS

There are spawners inside most mineshafts, so make sure you have good weapons and armor. You can also place four torches around the spawner to stop it from working while you destroy it.

NETHER SAY NEVER

Build the ultimate nether base with redstone defenses

NETHER BASE

Difficulty:
TRICKY

THIS BUILD USES
SOME TRICKY
TECHNIQUES BUT
IS WORTH IT.
Time needed:
3–4 HOURS

EXTRA INFO:
Build yourself
an obsidian
panic room.

1

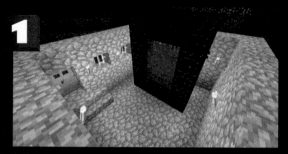

SECURE YOUR PORTAL

Before you even start your base, you've got to make sure your portal can't be blown up by ghasts. So, first off, make sure you completely surround it with a cobblestone room. Yes, even the floor needs to be made of stone.

2

DOUBLE SECURITY

Using iron doors will help keep you safe, but using two is even better. Build a short hallway by your first door, then place a second one. This way if you get followed in, then you'll have a second chance to escape. It's good to plan ahead!

3

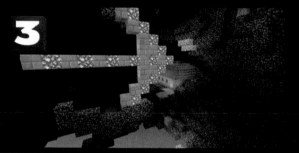

MARK YOUR WAY

Lots of the Nether looks largely the same, so make sure to use big markers to track where you placed your portal. There's nothing worse than trying to run away from a horde of zombie pigmen and getting lost in the process!

4

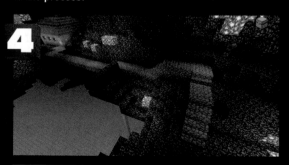

HARD PATH

Netherack explodes if it gets hit by ghast fire, so to stop the risk of the ground beneath you suddenly disappearing and falling into lava, be sure to build some stone paths wherever you go. This hard path will be more secure.

INSPIRATION

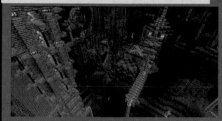

HOT STACK Using lava to make stone alters is really fine work from t3h0nly1.

STAR WARS Unadorned recreated the spot where Obi-Wan fought Anakin.

SET SAIL Linard's boat is completely made of stone so it won't burn on the lava.

5

SAFE HOUSES

Now and then, it's wise to build a ghast-proof safe house. Make your walls 3x3 and two-high, with ladders at one end. Leave a blank layer so you can see out and shoot arrows, then put a roof on top.

6

SMALL FOUNDATIONS

You want the rooms of your base to be quite small so ghasts don't spawn inside. Dig a one-deep hole and make it 7x12 wide. Then fill it in with stone or nether brick. Never use wood—it'll only set on fire.

7

WALLED IN

Build your walls with any brick you like (except wood) but only make them four high to deter ghasts. Create holes where you want windows and use iron bars in place of glass to give it a tough look.

8

STEP UP

Make your door one level higher than normal so that if monsters try to follow you, the extra step will buy you a little bit of time. Use the double door design from Step 2 as well, just for extra security.

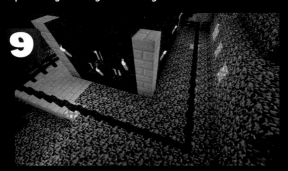

9

PROTECT THE PERIMETER

Make it harder for zombie pigmen to follow you by creating a border two to three blocks away from your base out of netherack or cobblestone fence. That way they won't surprise you as you step outdoors.

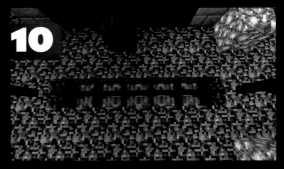

10

RISING POSTS

Now we're going to make it so that fence will rise up behind you from the safety of your base. Dig a two-deep hole along your fence border, and put sticky pistons along the bottom with fence posts on top.

11

WIRING

Now dig up the space in front of your base to place the wires. Place a repeater behind each piston, and then redstone dust behind the repeaters. This is all looking pretty fiendish!

12

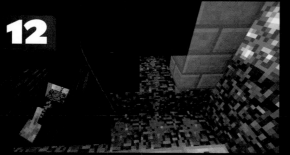

CONTROLLED INSIDE

Dig a path into your house. Since it's not deep down, you can just make the blocks step up and then cover them with redstone dust. Now place a lever to make your redstone work.

13

COVER UP

Hide all of your wiring with stone blocks, and a slab for the point where it leads into your base. Now nothing can get to it and break it, even if it was trying really hard to sabotage your stronghold.

INSPIRATION

HELL'S PALACE This smart build by Abycia looks like the perfect Demon King's lair.

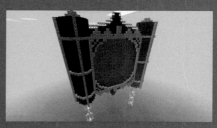

PORTAL POWER TheBigCactus works from the outside in, making an excellent portal.

CASTLE CRASHERS You'd be safe from harm in this fort by SamhatesJam.

14

PANIC ROOM

Finally, create a room completely made of obsidian directly beneath your base with a trapdoor and ladder entrance. If all other security fails, you'll be able to hide in here safely. Phew!

MINECRAFT VS. REAL LIFE

Let the battle for the best reality commence . . .

Minecraft teaches you important skills like creativity, spatial awareness, survival, and teamwork. People have created things that would be impossible in real life – huge roller coasters, works of art, and technological wonders. Others have explored avenues that would be far too expensive in real life, like building a supercomputer or a giant golden statue of themselves. Minecraft gives you all of this and more. But there are so many other ways that Minecraft beats real life . . .

1 PETS

In real life, there's always some kind of barrier to owning your very own pony/cat/dog—having to look after it, mostly. Minecraft has no such barriers. If you can tame it, you can keep it—but Minecraft doesn't stop there. Why have a regular cow when you can have . . . a mushroom cow? Real life: 0 Minecraft: 1.

2 BEING RICH

It's pretty hard to get rich in Minecraft, but nowhere near as hard as in real life. The only things holding you back in the blocky world are how much time and effort you're willing to put in—and if you're in Creative mode, you don't even have to put in as much time and effort because you already own all the diamonds you could ever want. We guess that makes them worthless, but still: diamonds!

3 ALONE TIME

There are many times in life where you just want to be left alone, but you have to see family and come downstairs from your room. Not so in Minecraft, where you can build yourself a giant wall or dig down into your own private bunker so you never, ever have to see another person again. The ultimate quiet response.

4 DREAM HOUSE

It's hard to get the perfect house in real life, unless you have wheelbarrows full of money and a mind-reading architect. Not so in Minecraft, where the power is in your hands. No planning permission, no worrying about costs, no forms to fill in, or nonsense at all! Awesome.

5
LOOK GREAT

There are no showers in Minecraft. You will never have to comb your hair. You don't even have to change your clothes. However, at any given moment, you can decide to be a completely different person by changing your skin—a celebrity, a tiger, Iron Man, a shoe—and there's almost no effort involved. Changing skins in real life is dangerous, and probably illegal.

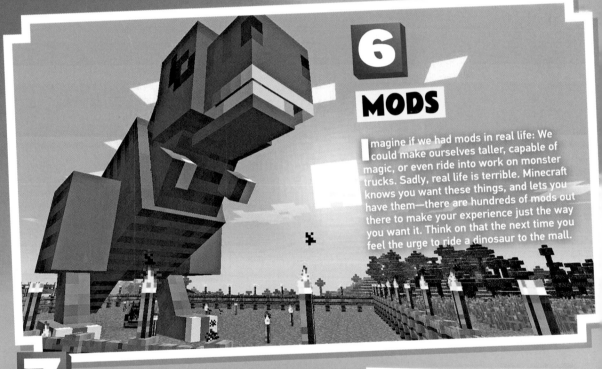

6
MODS

Imagine if we had mods in real life: We could make ourselves taller, capable of magic, or even ride into work on monster trucks. Sadly, real life is terrible. Minecraft knows you want these things, and lets you have them—there are hundreds of mods out there to make your experience just the way you want it. Think on that the next time you feel the urge to ride a dinosaur to the mall.

7
SAVING

If life had save points, nothing bad would ever happen. No one would ever lose their keys, go on bad dates, or get into fights—they'd just go back to an earlier save and do everything right. Sadly, life isn't so kind. But Minecraft is. If something you've spent hours on gets set on fire or blown up or infested with zombies, you can just save, reload, and try again. Easy.

8

FIGHTING

If you got into a brawl in real life, especially if it involved a diamond sword, you'd probably get into an awful lot of trouble—if not with the police, then with your parents/teachers at least. Minecraft is a much safer space to practice your swordplay, and your enemies are more likely to be bad guys like zombie pigmen and skeletons.

9

HEALING

In the real world, healing is a tricky thing: costly, time-consuming, and sometimes impossible, depending on the nastiness of the injury. In Minecraft, you can fall off a cliff and as long as you've got some bread in your pockets, you'll be just fine in a matter of minutes! Seriously, don't try this at home. Bread cannot fix broken bones. No, neither can cake. Behave.

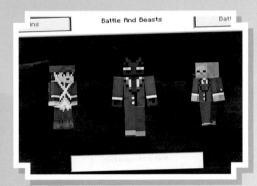

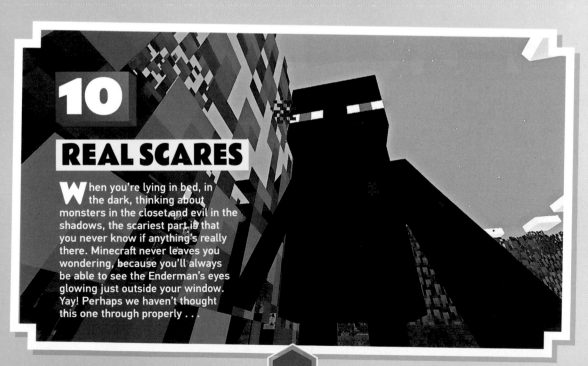

10

REAL SCARES

When you're lying in bed, in the dark, thinking about monsters in the closet and evil in the shadows, the scariest part is that you never know if anything's really there. Minecraft never leaves you wondering, because you'll always be able to see the Enderman's eyes glowing just outside your window. Yay! Perhaps we haven't thought this one through properly . . .

BUILD A SPOOKY GHOST TRAIN

It's Halloween, here's how to give your pals a real fright!

INFO

GHOST TRAIN
Difficulty:
HARD
BUT WORTH
EVERY SECOND
SPENT GETTING
IT RIGHT!

Time needed:
1 HOUR

EXTRA INFO:
Who's going to ride
your ghost train?
Put in what will
scare them most!

A round Halloween, what could be better than designing your own terrifying fairground ride? It's a bit of a challenge, but once you actually get this adapted minecart ride working, you'll be glad you took the time. And you can experiment with adding your own personal nightmares to the creepiness within! Let's get started . . . hold someone's hand if you're too scared to do it on your own!

IN THE BEGINNING
To keep a minecart moving, you need to use a powered rail, which needs a redstone torch nearby to power it. Another thing to keep in mind, don't use powered rails or detector rails on corners. They won't work and your cart could just stop.

ATOP THE MOUNTAIN
Grab red, white, and black wool; redstone blocks; and white and red terracotta. Start by dropping a row of eight red wool for the bottom lip. From here, add in black and white for the mouth. Add an upper lip, then fill in the skin with terracotta.

3

BRAIN DEAD

Now add in the white sides and continue the mouth. Drop in the hair on both sides with red wool, then grab end blocks and end bricks for the creepy brain on top. For the back of the head, fill in with white terracotta. Fingers are optional!

4

NOW THE TRACK

Knock out two blocks vertically from the face. Head on into the creative menu and equip nether brick. Now build a staircase from the mouth to ground level. Add rails and powered rails and give it a quick test to see if it works.

5

MORE TRACK

If your minecart made it all the way up, then you're safe to move on to building more track. Mine through the head to the other side. Run a row of tracks and then build the track upward at the end. Continue around to the right by around 10 blocks.

6

RIDE THE TRACK

Take a ride and see where the cart falls. There, place four tracks behind the point of impact and work your way forward. Continue down the mountainside and around to the front with the intention of building into the front of the mountain.

7

GHASTLY!

Dig a two-high, seven-long cave. Turn the end of the corridor into a five-wide room. Add in rows of dispensers on both sides, then dig a trench below the dispensers. Add stone above the dispensers, place detector rails in the middle then fill with ghasts!

8

ZOMBIE JUMP SCARE

Dig out a 3x3 hole four blocks deep. In the center, dig a block and place an upward-facing sticky piston. Lay a block on top, then soul sand. Finally, drop an armor stand on top of that and watch as it mysteriously sinks.

SPOOKY NIGHT

Add armor and a head. Place soul sand on top, then place a piston facing down above that. Next, grab redstone and place it next to that. What should happen is the soul sand is pushed into the armor stand. Now remove the piston and redstone.

GRAVE ERROR

In front, on the ground, drop redstone dust. Trail it on to a step, then up and under where your track will go. Use a lever to test it, and if it works, change the lever for a detector rail. Finish off with grass, coal, and half slabs for tombtones.

ZOMBIE SCARES

Make sure you have a four-block-gap between zombie scares, and don't forget to place the detector rails on top of the final redstone dust. If you used these in another build, substitute the detector rail for a pressure plate and they'll work.

LAVA-LY STUFF

Continue the track along by digging a two-high corridor. Mine up the walls then dig a one-block trench – floor and ceiling. At the end of the corridor, create a step leading up. Now go back to the two trenches and fill them with lava!

SLIME TIME

Continue up from the step to ground level. Add a corner turn at the top so the track leads out to the left. At the end, add slime with an upward-facing piston below. Place redstone below and trail it to a detector block. The minecart will jump on the slime!

MORE TRACK

Where the minecart lands, place nether bricks with a rail on. Add a straight, then a big climb. Drop in another straight, a turn, and then one more straight. deck it out with powered rails and, like always, give it a test run.

15

GOING UNDERGROUND

Having built the track high, let the minecart ride off and where it lands, dig a three-wide hole 15 blocks deep. Make sure you put rails just in front in case your cart doesn't land flush. Now comes an eerie hallway that's sunken into the earth.

16

THE SECRET ROOM

A five-wide hallway is next. Replace walls with quartz blocks (half slabs for the ceiling). Change the floor to planks and hang paintings. Create two tables, add a sea lantern to the ceiling, and make a two-high window in the center of the end wall.

17

MORE OF THE SAME

Around the corner, create another small room on the right. There's a lot of repetition to go through here, just to make your ghost train full of detail! Add another armor stand (with armor and a head) and place a door in front of it.

INSPIRATION

HALLOWE'EN MINE CART

TheGeekBarbie showed off this epic creation on YouTube.

MINECRAFT GHOST TRAIN

Great job by David Crotty Nangle on his spooky train!

MAD HOUSE

Tom Weller took a slightly different scary route, see it on YouTube!

18

DOOR SLAM

In the center of the hallway outside, dig down and lay redstone dust that leads to a redstone torch directly under the door. Add a pressure plate to test, and the door should slam shut when you approach it.

19 ANOTHER CORRIDOR

Place two crafting tables with a redstone torch on top, then turn to the left and create a front door area. Add an armor stand to the right to look like a coatrack then a plant on the left. All this is to lull the rider into a false sense of security!

20 SCREAM FOR SPEED

At the end of the corridor, dig a four-block-long trench. Place three downward-facing dispensers and fill with ghasts. Now place TNT around the dispensers, cover over with wood, lay in detector rails, and this ride is sure to end with a bang!

There's no ghost train that can scare a spider jockey!

Let's build it!

FALLING FLOOR TRAP

Curiosity will kill the cat! Or anyone else who's nosy!

INFO

FALLING FLOOR TRAPS

Difficulty:
EASY

As long as your foes are easily fooled . . .

Time needed:
30 MINS

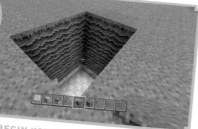

START HERE

1 BEGIN YOUR nasty scheme by digging up a three-block-wide trench. Ours is seven blocks in length, but you can make it as short or as long as you want. Next, dig the trench downward so you've got a nice big, death-inflicting drop. Those nosy enemies won't know what's hit 'em!

2 ON THE FAR SIDE, from ground level, dig three blocks down into the wall. Place a stone block in the center of the gap with a downward-facing piston directly above. Now drop a block with a lever, and place signposts as shown, coming off the stone. Rub your hands in glee (optional).

3 YOU SHOULD hopefully be left with a one-block gap underneath your piston contraption. Now when someone pulls the lever, the block will move and break the signpost bridge. If you want to turn this into a nasty lava trap, add two layers of lava at the bottom of the pit.

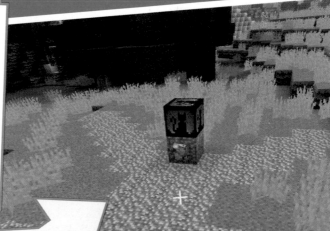

4 NOW ALL THAT'S LEFT is to add a falling block, like gravel, above the signs so when the piston breaks the bridge, the blocks all fall. To make the trap look less out of place, feel free to drop a redstone lamp above the lever block and build the gravel out so it looks completely natural.

BUILD THIS!

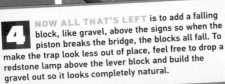

ANCIENT TEMPLE

Make a massive Minecraft monument on your map!

INFO

ANCIENT TEMPLE
Difficulty:
MEDIUM

Time needed:
5 HOURS

EXTRA INFO:
It's huge! Halve
the lengths for
a small one

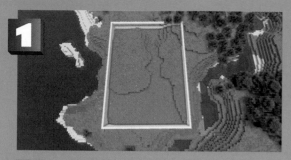

1 PLATFORM ONE

Find a really big, flat area to build upon. You'll need lots of space for this one. Use quartz to mark out an area that's 48 wide and 64 long. Make it four high and fill in the sides.

2 STEP UP

Use more quartz to make a border four wide on each side, then mark where your next layer will be. It's also four high and should be 40 wide and 56 blocks long. Now fill in the sides.

3 BASE FINISH

The last step of the base is another four blocks in and four blocks high. It's 32 wide and 48 long. This time fill in the top completely—this will be the floor for your temple build.

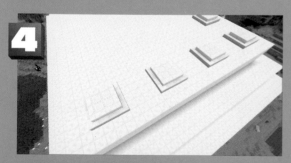

4 FOUNDATIONS

Now it's time to get the pillars in place. Use pillar quartz in 2x2 squares, with a ring of quartz steps all the way around. They are two blocks in from the corner, then four blocks apart on the sides.

INSPIRATION

INSIDE COURTYARD

Agne28 extends their temple further by adding more buildings.

GRAND SCALE

The colors of Wahar's impressive temple look impressively regal!

SIAMESE TEMPLE

There's some really cool Eastern inspiration for west2554's build.

5

GOING UP

Check that all of your pillars line up before you start building them up—there should be four on the short sides and six on the long sides. Now build the pillars up so that they're 16 blocks high.

6

STANDING TALL

Continue building all of your pillars so they're all 16 blocks tall. Then put a ring of upside-down stairs around the top of each one. It's really starting to look like a temple now!

7

RAISE THE ROOF

Take out some chiseled quartz blocks for the roof. Make it overhang by two blocks around all the edges. It should be 32x48 like the top giant step. Fill the whole thing in.

8

TURN A CORNER

Now that all of the big parts are done, we can move on to start the decorations! In each corner of the roof, place pillar quartz two wide with chiseled quartz on top. But leave the corner bare.

9

TRIMMINGS

Now we'll make a border all the way around. Going one in from your corners, swap between blue-stained clay and yellow-stained clay to this pattern. Now repeat this on every side.

10

ROOF EDGE

Make the roof edges on the short sides. Start one block in from the edge with quartz stairs, two quartz blocks, then upside-down stairs. Repeat the pattern and make it go up.

11

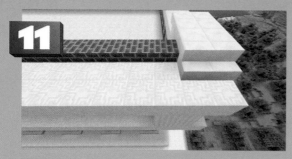

START TILING

Make the roof edge pattern again so that it's two deep. Now get loads of brick slabs. Start two blocks in and start laying down slabs. Step half a space up for each line of roof.

12

FILL IT IN

The top layer of the roof is four blocks wide – the whole thing should be quite shallow. Once it's all filled in, add a quartz slab and some stairs onto the front edges as decoration.

13

DECORATIONS

Now to decorate the two ends! You can do whatever you like, but we've gone for some pillars and a small flower design with chiseled quartz background. Maybe try a creeper face.

INSPIRATION

GARDEN TOO

The outside is just as grand as the temple itself. Thanks Tombuis!

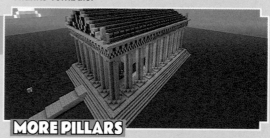

MORE PILLARS

This build is absolutely packed with detail from Kaufenll.

MAYAN PYRAMID

A different take on a classic temple, thanks mycastke2!

14

STAIRWAY

The final touch is some stairs at the front to get in! Use quartz steps four wide to reach the top, then make a border of pillar quartz with more steps on top to make it neat. Now you're finished!

TRAVEL FASTER

Using water in mob farms can make things easier, but if you then put ice underneath the water, you'll make things travel even faster.

FLAME-PROOF

Wooden planks catch fire easily, but wooden slabs don't. If there's lava nearby and you don't have any cobblestone, try using slabs instead.

ULTIMATE SURVIVAL TIPS!

Our quick tips to give you the edge in survival mode

MINE SMARTER

Need to clear loads of sand or gravel but your spade is about to break? Use a torch to burn through a pile instead. Simply knock out the bottom block, then quickly place a torch underneath and it will break the whole stack in seconds.

TAKE A BREATHER

Not sure how to explore underwater to see those ocean monuments without drowning? Take loads of ladders or signs with you—you can use them to make air pockets to catch your breath during long dives. Guardian fights, here we come!

I really should get some armor . . .

THE GOLDEN RULE

Always take a chest with you when you're exploring. You don't want to lose all of those items you've spent so long collecting—better keep them safe, just in case a stray skeleton arrow takes you down.

HOLD IT IN

Weirdly, pressure plates can be used to hold in blocks of lava or water, even if you step on them—great for decorating, or when you're trying to clear a safe path in a mine.

STEPPING STONES

When you first find a village, not every house will be usable. Some need a helping hand before a villager can use it to hide in. Check every house to see if it needs stairs to get up to, or if the door is blocked.

EVERYTHING YOU NEED TO KNOW ABOUT VILLAGES!

Seven top tips to making village life work for you!

Hey, witch, what's your best subject in school?

CHEAP UPGRADE

If you want villagers to breed, you'll need to build more houses with doors. But you might be able to get a few extra really easily. The small square buildings often spawn without doors, so just put one on, and more villagers can breed.

PIT FALLS

Villages often spawn above or near caverns full of nasty mobs that come out at night. Your residents will keep falling into them, too, so rescue any villagers that have fallen in, then fill in the holes so that they don't get stuck again!

TRADING

Having lots of villagers is great for trading to get items that are hard to find in your area. If you keep trading, you can get rarer items. Sadly, you can't trade in Pocket Edition yet.

GUARDIAN FORCES

You can't always be around to help your villagers, so spawning an Iron Golem as a bodyguard will really help! They'll either spawn if you have 10 villagers and 21 doors, or you can make your own.

TRANSFORMATIONS

If a zombie attacks a villager, there's a good chance it will turn into a dangerous zombie villager and attack you too. You can even find whole villages of nothing but zombies! Also be careful during lightning storms. If lightning strikes a villager, it will turn into a witch!

Why, it's spelling, of course!

FARMER'S HAND

If you want a helping hand with your farms, then expanding the ones in the villages are a good idea. The villages will tend to them like they belong to them.

HOW TO DEFEAT SKELETONS

Our Minecraft Experts show you the best way . . .

WHACKING TIME!

If you're in a cave, chances are you've got a selection of random blocks, probably dirt or cobblestone. If you meet a skeleton, build a two-high, three-wide wall and hide behind the middle. The skeleton will come after you. When it does, it'll be within whacking distance.

NO RUNNING

Never run directly at a skeleton unless you want to die incredibly fast. Instead, try to zigzag toward them. Running either left-and-forward or right-and-forward means the arrows will be shot at where you were, rather than where you are.

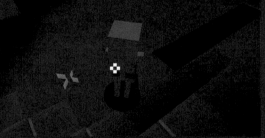

READY FIGHT!

Skeletons normally have the upper hand in a fight. If you see it first, you can win with some clever thinking. When spotted, mine up so you're above it but not so high you'll take damage. Line it up, then divebomb onto the skeleton while swinging your sword.

CREEPER POWER

How often has a creeper ended your run? Time to turn the tables! If you see a skeleton in the same area as a creeper, aggravate the creeper. Make it follow you so it's near the skeleton, and when it starts flashing, run off as it blows itself and the skeleton up.

LAVA LAVA FUN

This one requires you to be ready to run like your feet are on fire. Always carry a bucket of lava with you, you know . . . for safety. Then, when a skeleton shows its pearly white face, dump the bucket at its feet and run like your life depended on it (because it does!).

EIGHT IS BETTER THAN ONE

The only thing better than one wolf is two wolves. Better yet, why not tame an entire pack? Having eight or so wolves at your disposal makes you a force to be reckoned with. Just slap the skeleton once and sit back as your pack literally picks the bones.

MOB RULE

While mobs don't naturally attack one another, no mob enjoys being turned into a pincushion. It's possible to kill skeletons by moving back so another mob is in between you and the skeleton. When the skeleton shoots the mob, the mob will turn on ol' boney face.

RUN AWAY!

There's no shame in running away from a fight. When you get hit by an arrow, turn and run until you're safely around a corner. Then all you need to do is lie in wait until the skeleton ventures around the corner after you. It will now be within whacking distance.

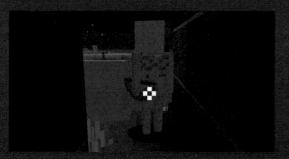

DIG FOR VICTORY!

The other safest way to close the gap and get within whacking distance without losing health is to dig around the skeleton. By that, we mean dig into the nearest wall and along the side of where the skeleton is. When you're near, mine out and start whacking!

TAKE A BOW

Bows are the best weapons against most mobs. They allow you to keep a distance between yourself and the target while also keeping an eye on the battlefield. Knowing which mob is where and adjusting your plan will offer better results than blindly charging in.

HAUNTED HOUSE!

Build a creepy home for your friends to visit!

MAKING SHAPES

Lay your foundations and put in a floor so it's all flat to build from. The whole area is a 15x15 square, but make your building an L shape with some outside space to make it more interesting.

BUILD YOUR WALLS

You want the first-floor walls to be five blocks high because tall ceilings feel creepier. Use cobblestone for the bottom layer and planks for the others, with tree trunks in each of the corners for texture.

GOING UP

After adding in some windows it's time to build a second floor. Use tree trunks to show the change in floors, and then use planks for your walls. We made this layer four blocks high.

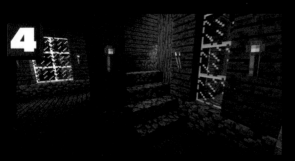

STEP UP

Add in a staircase to get to your upper floor. Make it twist and hide it with a wall so it feels dark and scary. Use redstone torches for light as they're darker than normal ones.

INSPIRATION

CREEPSHOW JarY's classic spook house looks like a haunted hotel from the movies!

DEVIL HORNS With its tusks and towers, Dalaxys's house just screams "Run away!"

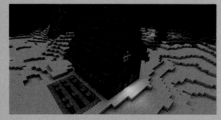

SPOOK SHACK Everyone knows the littlest haunts are the scariest, eh, Ender Lord 333!

5

COVER UP

Use stairs to make a simple stepping-up roof with planks on top. Make sure it sticks out on all sides by one block. We tested stone and dark oak, but chose the wood in the end!

6

COME TOGETHER

Start with the roof edges, including the small part of your L to make sure it all lines up when it joins. The small part won't be as high as the main roof. Now give your attic a few windows.

7

SECRET WALL

Now it's time to decorate! You can make a secret path using a large painting by making a 1x2 block walkway and using signposts to trick the painting into thinking it's a solid wall.

8

HOME SWEET HOME

It's still a house even if it is haunted, so adding some chairs and maybe a coffee table will keep it feeling more like a home. Make it creepy by adding cobwebs and the weird clown painting.

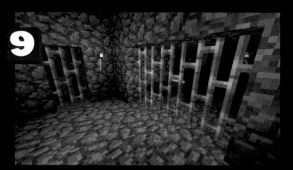

9

DAMP CELLAR

No haunted house worth its salt is complete without a scary basement, so you'd better dig a small room underneath your house. Add some prison cells using iron bars for extra creepiness!

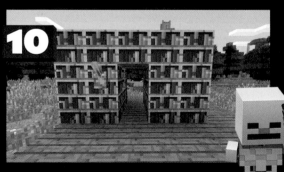

10

REDSTONE BOOKCASE

It wouldn't be a haunted house without a secret passage hidden by a bookcase! We're showing it outside to make it easy to see, but be sure to put yours in a dark corner of your house.

11

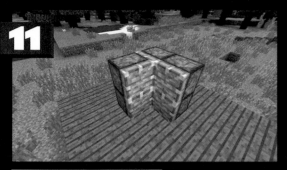

SOMETHING STICKY

You'll need six sticky pistons – four facing out to the side, and then two that face toward where you want your secret door to be. Put some bookshelves in front of the visible sticky parts.

12

CIRCUITRY

Place wool around the top of your pistons to make it easy to see your circuit. Put redstone dust along the top and a repeater set to two or three on top of your back piston. Now test it with a lever.

INSPIRATION

FOREST FEAR Fancepants proves that a spooky house is spookier with woods!

FRIGHT HOUSE Starferret goes one better and gives us a massive haunted mansion!

TERROR TOWERS This dark and imposing build by GreyHavens gives us the shivers!

13

HIDE AWAY

Use more cases for the sides of your path and put redstone dust along them until it's behind the front bookcase. It's enough to activate it so you can put your lever here. Now cover it all up!

14

SMASH IT UP

The last step is to make the place look old and abandoned. Smash windows, place cobwebs, and swap stairs for planks to make it look like bits of wall are missing. You want messy rather than neat here!

Are you okay? You're looking a bit stiff . . .

MINECRAFT AND THE LOST THRONE ROOM

Create a mysterious statue down in the murky depths . . .

INFO

LOST THRONE ROOM
Difficulty: **MEDIUM**
Time needed: **3 HOURS**
EXTRA INFO: It all looks a bit blue until you use the sponge.

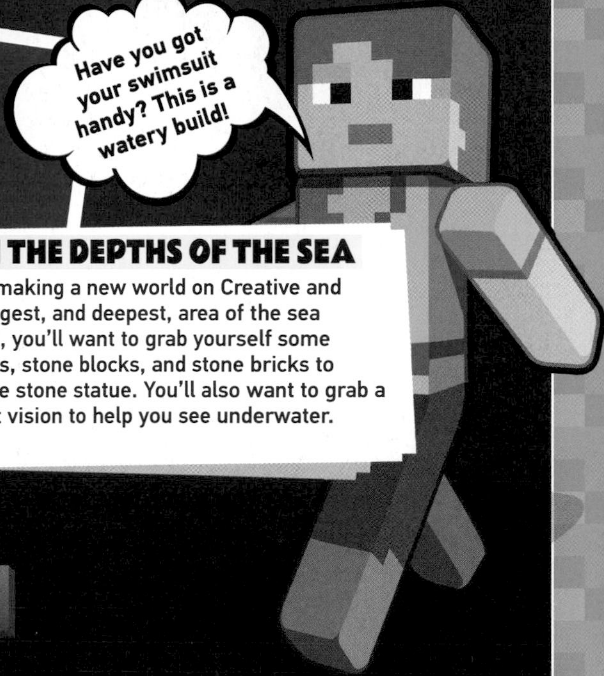

Have you got your swimsuit handy? This is a watery build!

1

DOWN IN THE DEPTHS OF THE SEA

Let's start by making a new world on Creative and finding the biggest, and deepest, area of the sea possible. Next, you'll want to grab yourself some chiseled blocks, stone blocks, and stone bricks to create a simple stone statue. You'll also want to grab a potion of night vision to help you see underwater.

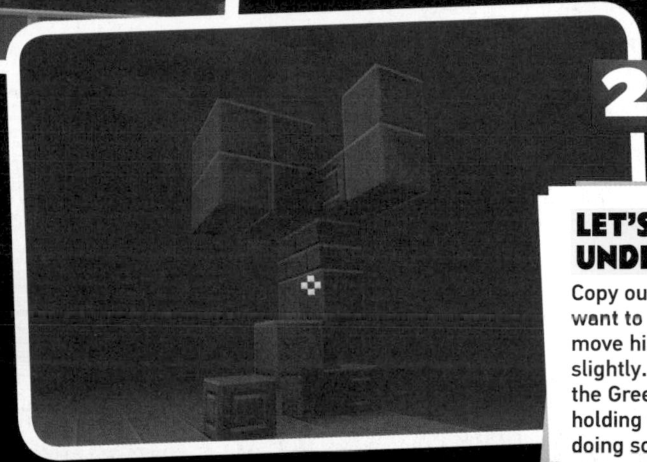

2

LET'S BUILD AN UNDERWATER STATUE . . .

Copy our statue here. With it built you'll want to extend his arms upward and move his legs so it looks like he's kneeling slightly. This statuesque man is Atlas, the Greek Titan who was charged with holding up the sky. But for us, he'll be doing something different . . .

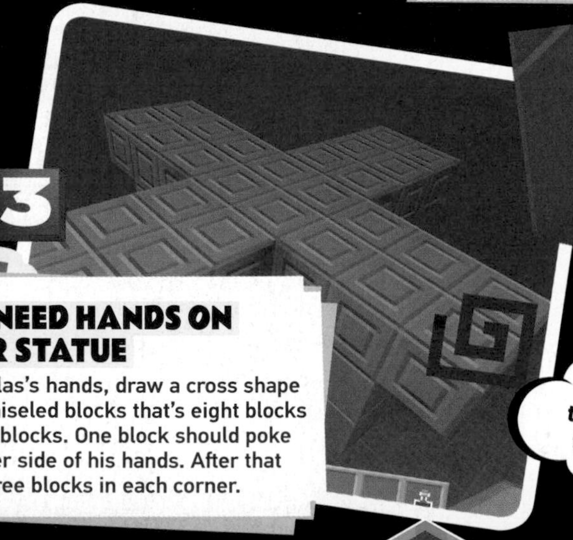

3

YOU NEED HANDS ON YOUR STATUE

From Atlas's hands, draw a cross shape out of chiseled blocks that's eight blocks by eight blocks. One block should poke out either side of his hands. After that place three blocks in each corner.

Stretch . . . two, three, four. Up . . . two, three, four!

4

TIME FOR FUN WITH TURRETS

Now we're going to grab our stone bricks and build the walls up three high, then drop on another layer of chiseled blocks on top and fill in the corner gaps. After, place another row of stone bricks on top around the outside, then on every side that's four blocks long, build it up another one block to create a castle's turret effect. Finally, place another row of chiseled blocks around the bottom, and you've got yourself a castle turret that's being held in place by Atlas himself!

5

FOUR IS BETTER THAN ONE!

Up next, we need to build another Atlas and castle turret to the left of this one. Ours is 20 blocks away, but you can make it as small or as large as you like. After that, build another two Atlas+turret combos to create the four base pillars of the sunken castle. When finished, let's connect all four turrets with stone bricks surrounded by chiseled blocks. In Greek mythology, there was only one Atlas. But this isn't Greek mythology, so we're going to end up with four! If you're after a simple pattern to break up the boring gray of the stone wall, try making a glass cross shape enclosed in stone blocks.

LET'S MESS THIS PLACE UP

Find the rough center of the first wall and smash it to bits. This is where the drawbridge would have been had the city not fallen into ruins. But where is the drawbridge now? Why, it's fallen to pieces on the seabed! Placing blocks messily can create the illusion of something that's been badly damaged. In this case, it's a drawbridge. You could also break parts off some of the turrets to make them look even more broken.

6

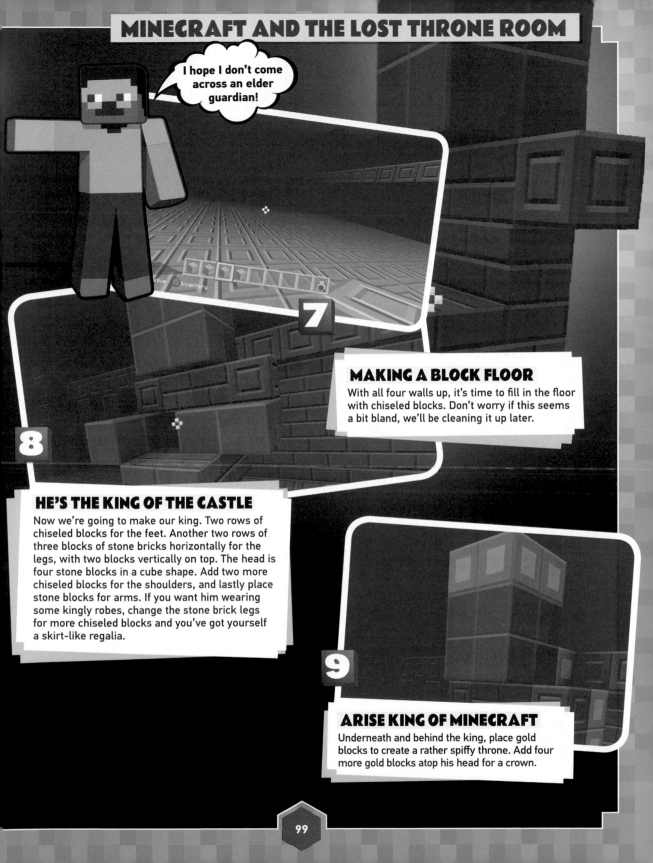

I hope I don't come across an elder guardian!

7

8

MAKING A BLOCK FLOOR

With all four walls up, it's time to fill in the floor with chiseled blocks. Don't worry if this seems a bit bland, we'll be cleaning it up later.

HE'S THE KING OF THE CASTLE

Now we're going to make our king. Two rows of chiseled blocks for the feet. Another two rows of three blocks of stone bricks horizontally for the legs, with two blocks vertically on top. The head is four stone blocks in a cube shape. Add two more chiseled blocks for the shoulders, and lastly place stone blocks for arms. If you want him wearing some kingly robes, change the stone brick legs for more chiseled blocks and you've got yourself a skirt-like regalia.

9

ARISE KING OF MINECRAFT

Underneath and behind the king, place gold blocks to create a rather spiffy throne. Add four more gold blocks atop his head for a crown.

I think this king is a real drip!

10

GUARDS FOR KINGLY PROTECTION

A king needs his guards. So now we'll build two statues guarding him similar to how we built Atlas, only with one arm extended for later. With that complete, dig up a hole in the floor to make a window into the sea floor below.

11

KEEP THE WATER OUT

We're now going to need to waterproof the inside. Grab some glass blocks and place a row around the outside of the structure. Afterward, build one block in and place another row. Continue this another two more times, then fill in the rest of the dome with a flat glass formation. Completing this only leaves the door . . .

12

SOAK UP THE WATER

Head back to the main door and place two columns in the middle and signs along the left and right sides to stop water coming in. And here's the fun part: Grab some sponge and place it everywhere inside until you've soaked up all the water. It'll look like a big mess, but you can mine all the sponge once it's water-free.

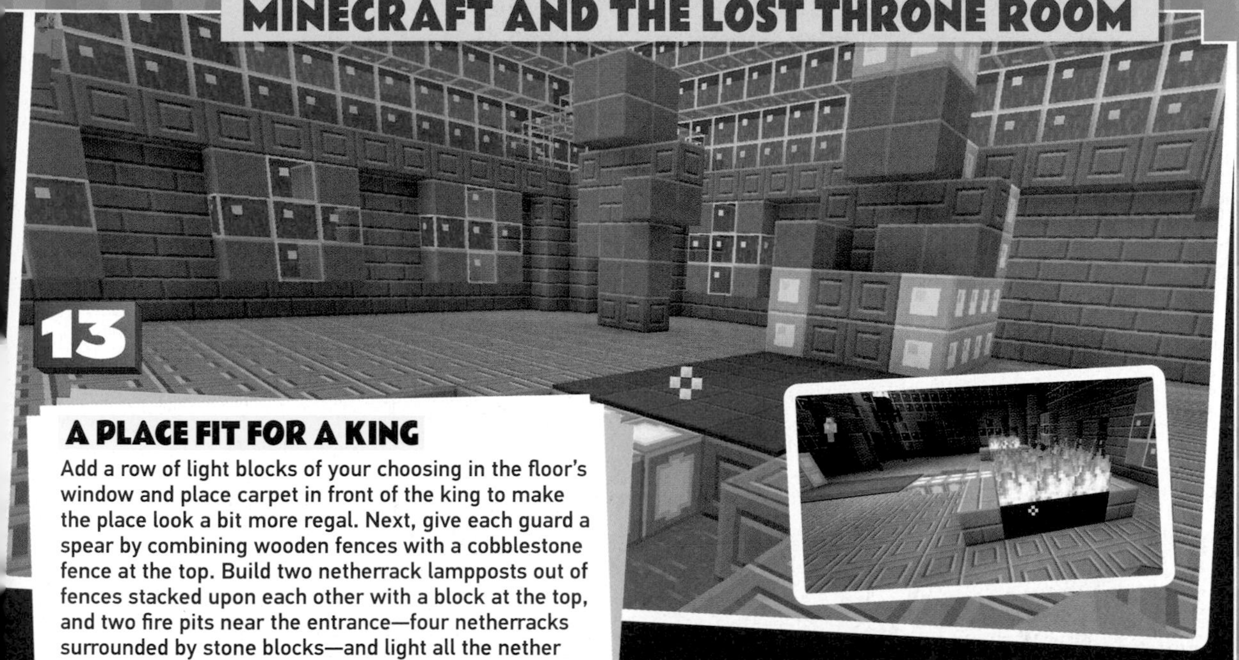

13

A PLACE FIT FOR A KING

Add a row of light blocks of your choosing in the floor's window and place carpet in front of the king to make the place look a bit more regal. Next, give each guard a spear by combining wooden fences with a cobblestone fence at the top. Build two netherrack lampposts out of fences stacked upon each other with a block at the top, and two fire pits near the entrance—four netherracks surrounded by stone blocks—and light all the nether bricks with a flint and steel.

14

SHOW THEM THE WAY

All that's left to do now is head back to shore and create a statue to let people know there's a city underwater behind it (we made a winged statue) and place some light blocks about underwater to light up where it's a bit dark. You could even leave a light trail coming from the statue to the city. Maybe only place one or two near Atlas so the structure stays dark for a super-creepy feel.

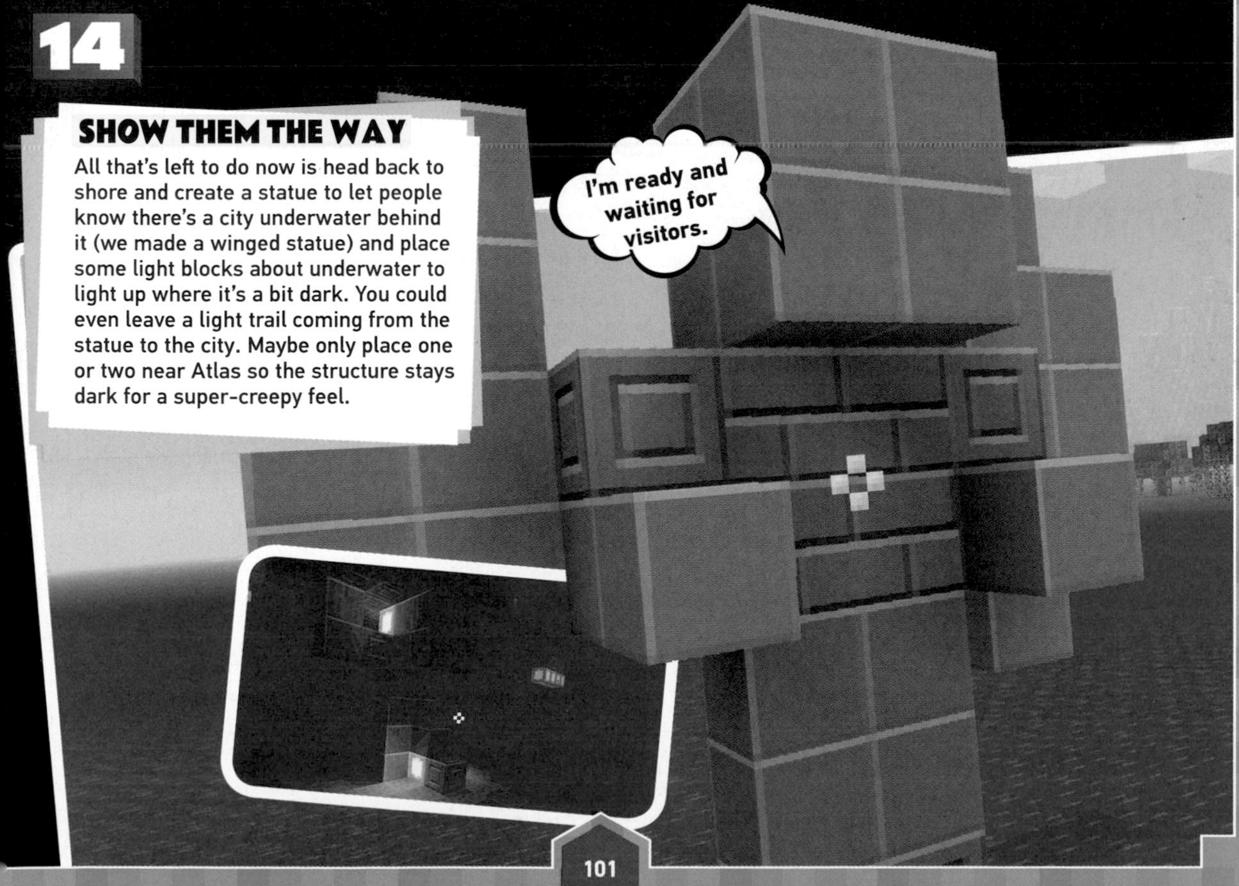

I'm ready and waiting for visitors.

You're a wizard at Minecraft! Create your own Wizard's Tower with our step-by-step guide . . .

BUILD A WIZARD'S TOWER

INFO

WIZARD'S TOWER

Difficulty:
HARD

THIS IS A BIG BUILD AND WILL TAKE YOU QUITE A WHILE.

Time needed:
1¾ HOURS

1 THE CIRCLE OF LIFE

Build a circle formation into the floor. The dimensions are seven, two, one, two, seven, two, one, two, seven, two, one, two, seven, two, one, two. If it's easier to remember, each quarter is seven, two right, one block, turn, then two blocks. Repeat the last part four times for a circle.

2 BUILD IT UP

For this next step, go and build all the sides up by 20 blocks. That may not seem like much, but this is the first level of our tower. Once that's completed, head to the top and count one block in. Run a ring of stone bricks around the inside of the top of the structure.

3

IN AND OUT

Build our middle section up by 10 blocks. Take a step back, you should see a clear dip where the tower goes in. Run a ring around the top of the second level that's one block out—just like in step one, only on top of the second section. With the new ring in, build it up by 20 blocks.

4

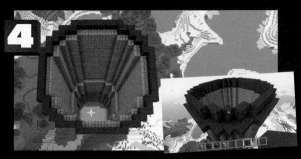

PURPLE RING PURPLE RING

Now let's start working on the spire. Pull out some purple concrete and purple wool. With the concrete, create a ring one block out from the top of the tower. Next, create another ring one block in and above. Build this up so it's two blocks higher than the first ring.

5

TOPPING IT OFF

On the two-high sections, build more, only this time make each one a single block in. Do this on all four sides until they meet. Fill in the corners. When you get to the top, make a two-high spike with an ender rod on top. Use purple wool to add in lines leading into the middle.

6

BRANCHING OUT

Head to the left side of the highest level and find the middle. One block in from each side, lay down two rows of seven blocks. At the end of the rows, create a ring with each of the main lengths being five blocks, and only two diagonal blocks separating.

7

HOW TALL IS YOURS?

Where you placed the two rows during Step 6 will decide how tall your new tower should be. The way to work out how tall it should be is to head to the main tower and run a line of blocks from the highest stone bricks. Wherever the line ends above your ring is how tall this tower should be.

8

RINGS & ROWS

Head to the underside of the newest tower. One block in, build another ring around the inside. When that's done, build another row underneath so you're left with a two-high wall. Under that, build a ring that is one block in. Now fill in the underside so the bottom is flat.

FENCE IT IN

On each end of the flat side, on the section facing the main tower, drop down two 2-blocks-high spikes. Create two more 2-high spikes diagonally. Then two single blocks diagonally. Finally, two more 2-high spikes, horizontally into the building. Make each block two wide. Add a fence on the second block in on each side.

TOPPING THE MINI TOWER

Now all that's left to do on this mini tower is the spire, which is essentially the same as the main tower's, only built with single layers instead of doubles. Run a ring around the outside, then build more single layers heading upward until all the sides meet in the middle-top. Use purple wool to add in strips.

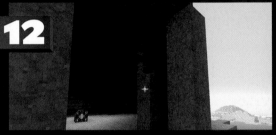

AND ANOTHER ONE

Repeat Steps 7-10 to create a second mini tower lower down on the front. Head to the tower and look at it from the front. This next tower starts from the top of the bottom part. To recap, you'll be building out, creating a ring, building the ring up, creating the underside, adding in the steps, the fencing, then making the spire.

OPEN THE GATE

Head to the bottom and smash in a six-high, four-wide door frame. Build the frame out of stone so it's three blocks in depth. Mine up the middle row on both sides and in the section above so you're left with a gap around the inside of the frame. Fill this gap with fences and in the center, build a two-high fence at the top.

THE WONDER OF WINDOWS

Keep your stone out because we'll be using it to build our windows, which look like glyphs (magic patterns) from a distance. The trick is to build all the glass sections one block back and the stone frame one block out. And be sure to add the windows to all four sides of the towers except for the sides with the walkways.

DOORS MARK THE SPOT

Another nice and easy one for you. On the walkways that lead to the mini towers, add doors at both ends. That's a total of four doors altogether, two on each walkway. These aren't essential, but if you ever build the interior, then the doors that lead to the inside will let you know where you'll need to connect your stairs.

15

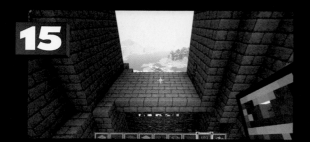

FINISHING TOUCHES

All that's left now is to create a lot of fireflies around the entire tower. Each one is made by placing a stone slab on the top and bottom of a block of glowstone. To get them all around at different heights, just build rows of blocks coming off the tower, then place your firefly at the end before smashing up all the rows.

INSPIRATION

CASTLE FALKENSTEIN
RobotChris has created an amazing medieval castle.

CASTLE ON THE MOUNTAIN
It's astonishing what Spakstor has produced here!

BEAST'S ENCHANTED CASTLE
Dennis Builds and Kellerbier's castle with rooms!

What do you mean? It looks nothing like Hogwarts!

ICE PALACE!

INFO

ICE PALACE
Difficulty:
MEDIUM-HARD
Time needed:
5 HOURS
EXTRA INFO:
This build is huge.
Keep things slim
and tall!

1

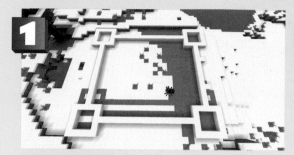

SNOW LINES

Find a snowy biome with a small hill. You want the front to face down the hill so make this 13 blocks wide, with two squares of 5x5 at either end. Then go 16 blocks back and put down more 5x5 squares.

2

ROYAL ENTRANCE

Make a fancy archway. Three blocks in from either side and one block in front of your blueprint, build a six-block-high pillar on each side. Step one in, and then go four up, then another block in a three up.

3

FIRST WALL

Build your first wall out of snow and make it 16 blocks high. Now knock out space for packed-ice windows one block on from the edge and three blocks up on both sides. They should be 10 blocks tall.

4

DARK PATH

Now complete the entrance using spruce wood and cobblestone blocks. Make a pattern that almost follows the archway, but smaller. This part lines up with your wall so it's behind your arch.

INSPIRATION

COOLFLUFFLE'S

amazing Glacier Palace is hugely complex construction to behold.

THIS ICY WONDER

by cschwalm was built using only five different kinds of blocks.

IT'S A PALACE!

And it's made of ice! Jerichiob10's build is totally see-through!

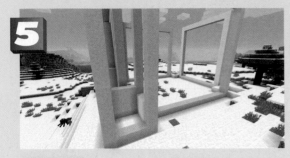

5

FRAMES

Since this is such a big build, it's a good idea to build frames for all of the walls to keep them the same height. Make all of the walls 16 blocks high, while the towers are even taller at 23 blocks high.

6

TOWER DEFENSE

On the two exposed sides, add packed-ice window decorations in the middle. Start six blocks up and make them 15 blocks tall. To add some ramparts go out one block around the top of each tower.

7

SIDE LINES

Next give the two sides a simple window design. One block in, and three blocks up, start making a packed ice window that's two wide and 10 tall. Make four of them with two blocks between each one.

8

BRING IT BACK

The wall at the very back should be your more decorative one, so you can go crazy here! We've gone for a framed diamond design, but you could also try crosses or arrows too. It's totally up to you!

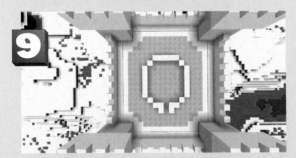

9

ON TOP

Now you have finished the main palace, be sure to have ramparts on every tower and at the top of each wall. Add a ceiling to your main hall, then lay plans down in a circle for the next tower stage!

10

SMALL BUT TALL

Try to copy your main building design in a near circle, only in mini form. Make your walls six blocks high, add packed-ice windows all around, and then add a mini arch to the front.

11

UP AGAIN

For the second layer, repeat the same design again in another six-block-high chunk with the same windows. Next, add some ramparts that stick out one block at the top.

12

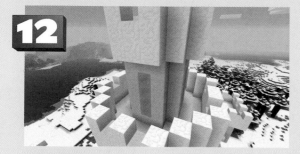

EVEN TALLER

Now for another layer! Go for a smaller circle in the middle and again make it six blocks high with windows. Add smaller ramparts to the top that stick out by one block.

13

MEGA VIEW

Now we're at the top, it's time for one last tower! This one is smaller and almost a square with small ramparts on top. You could go even taller if you like, but we think that this is high enough!

INSPIRATION

BLUESPARTAN

built their fabulously frosty ice palace on a snowy mountain top.

THERE'S AN

enormous load of blocks in Cameron224's amazing build. Cool!

LEOZAUR

had a go at replicating Elsa's ice palace from *Frozen*. Good job!

14

STAIRWAY

The final touch is some stairs at the front to get in! Use quartz steps four wide to reach the top, then make a border of pillar quartz with more steps on top to make it neat. Now you're finished!

HOW TO MAKE A SPLASH!

Build your own boat race!

INFO

BOAT RACE
Difficulty:
MEDIUM
Time needed:
2 HOURS
EXTRA INFO:
Try adding
branching paths.

1

PLAN YOUR ROUTE

After you've picked out a spot for your boat race ride, you'll need to roughly plot the area of the course. It can be as big or small as you want it to be, the bigger it is, the more time it'll take to build.

2

MAKE A CHANNEL

Once you know what rough path you want it to take, it's time to start making the track. Keep it six to eight blocks wide in most parts, but make it wider in others to give it variety. You'll need to dig a lot!

3

HAIRPIN BENDS

Tight corners like this one will add challenge to your course. Add one easily by making a straight path and add a rectangle to the side of it. Then delete the extra blocks and wall off the center.

4

JUMP START

Waterfalls make for an exciting beginning. Build a tower over your course and divide into two sections so you each have a spot to start in for your races. Then start adding some water.

INSPIRATION

A-MAZE-ING

Blitzgrutel's track is overflowing with different path choices.

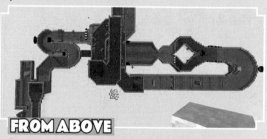

FROM ABOVE

Seeing guaja's track from the air is spectacular – loads of twists.

SLIDE AWAY

Who needs to race when you've got Ailtongn's huge waterslide?

SLIPPERY STAIRS

Mix it up by having watery stair slides as well as waterfalls. You'll just need to make a simple stair shape then pour more water over it. Make sure you have a border at the edges!

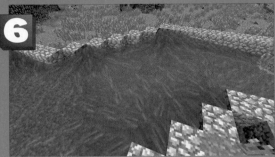

RIVER RAPIDS

Make waves by adding a bumpy water section. To do this, you'll need to place water a bit farther apart so it all crashes toward each other. Boats will need to be careful over this section.

SLIP AND SLIDE

Water travels faster over ice, so speed things up by putting ice under your track and then placing water over it. It can be the speedy part of your course—great for long straight sections.

IN THE DARK

You don't need to have everything above ground; you can add difficulty to your track by making a cave section so racers have to find their way around in the dark. A few torches may help.

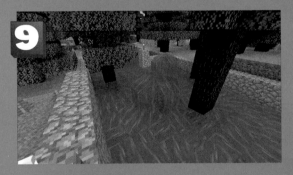

WATER SPOUTS

In wide areas, it's a good idea to keep things interesting by adding obstacles. Using blocks with more water on top makes mini fountains you have to dodge. Spawned mobs are also a fun idea.

KEEP IT NATURAL

Fit in to the surrounding area by making your track match your biome. Keep the local trees as obstacles in your course, and turn any higher walls into decorative waterfalls.

11

BUMPY RIDE

Every now and then, add a little drop of one or two blocks to help keep the speed of the race high. Mix up all of the sections you've used so far to keep the race exciting for all of the boats.

12

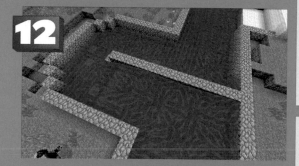

TIGHT CORNER

Remember the hairpin bend from earlier? It's time to tidy it up a bit. Add a curved edge so it's easier to turn around. Don't have too many rapids here, the corner will be tricky enough already.

INSPIRATION

LEAKY CEILING

Elmattol has waterfalls coming from the ceiling!

CLASSIC TRACKS

This track from karim007 keeps it simple . . .

DESERT DELIGHTS

Look at the decorations in JurreDam's theme!

13

FINISH LINE!

Create a wall with different colored wools to make a finish line. We've turned it into a landing area, but a fence over the top of the track will also work really well.

14

FINISHING TOUCHES

Go back to tidy up your course. Does your starting drop need to be bigger for boats? Does your track need more water? We added a building for riders to pick up boats too. Happy racing!

ESSENTIAL TERRAIN

Six important Minecraft structures to look for when exploring the world

You may be the only player in your Minecraft world, but there's plenty of seemingly man-made structures out there for you to find. Almost every biome can potentially hold these mysterious locations, but sometimes they can be hard to spot. Each one can house unimaginable riches and items as long as you know where to find them. Here are six Minecraft structures to look out for as you start to explore the expansive blocky lands.

1

DESERT PYRAMID

As you cross the desert biome, keep an eye out for pyramids. They're made of sandstone and the front has two towers. Underneath is a chest, but also some TNT - dig around it safely to break and collect the TNT, then open the chest and collect your goodies.

2

WOODLAND MANSION

Exclusive to dark forest biomes, woodland mansions are utterly enormous. These are hard to miss, because each one has multiple floors with a variety of different room types, some of which are concealed. Make sure you're breaking through walls to find secrets!

3

VILLAGE

One of the most common structures is a simple village. They can be found in six different biomes; plains, desert, taiga, savanna, snowy taiga, and snowy tundra. Villagers inhabit these and you can trade with most of them for emeralds.

4

OCEAN MONUMENT

If you fancy taking a dive into the deep blue, keep an eye out for monuments. Guardians defend every corner of them, but there's also some incredible loot. It's the only place you can find sponge blocks, and it's one of the only prismarine sources too.

5

NETHER FORTRESS

When you get around to building a portal to the Nether, look out for the intimidating nether fortresses. They're dark, tall, and full of enemies like wither skeletons and blazes. You'll need to make quite a few trips to them, however, if you want to brew any potions.

6

END CITY

When you slay the Ender Dragon, make sure you come back with an ender pearl. This will allow you to travel through a portal to a different area in the End dimension. Explore until you find an End City, which contains a lot of shulkers and some amazing loot.

Protect your bed from your mortal enemy while smashing theirs!

BED WARS

WHAT IS IT? This is a team survival game on the Hypixel network based around protecting your bed from the enemy and breaking other team's beds as quickly as you can. It's a bit like capture the flag.

HOW DO I WIN? Stand in your island's iron and gold generator to gather resources, which you can trade with Villagers for items that will help you in your battle. You win by killing everyone and destroying their beds.

EXPERT TIPS! Build to the diamond and emerald generators in the center of the map to obtain better items. Create protective layers around your bed with hard blocks that are difficult to destroy. Use water in your bed defenses to make life harder for enemies.

DID YOU KNOW? Bed Wars is now an official game on the Hypixel Network!

MULTIPLAYER GAME TIPS

Quick tips and hints to improve your PvP gaming!

Use blocks to build pathways to the center of the map—that's where the good stuff is!

SKY WARS

WHAT IS IT? Everyone in the game has their own pre-built island with three chests on it full of goodies. The key to winning the game is to build to the center of the map where there are more chests with better gear.

HOW DO I WIN? This is a game of Last Man Standing – so you just have to kill everyone else on the map! It's very easy to lose your footing and fall off the map into the void. Once you have obtained the good gear in the center, go around and pick off each target.

EXPERT TIPS! Use snowballs and eggs as a cheaper substitute to bows and arrows in your battles. They have the same knockback rating as arrows, but are much more common and can be thrown instantly. This will make it easier to knock people off into the void.

DID YOU KNOW? Sky Wars is officially the most popular PvP game on the Hypixel Network. We have often seen over 15,000 players battling it out on the server at the same time. Whoa!

TURBO KART RACERS

WHAT IS IT? You've played Mario Kart, right? This is Hypixel's own take on the go-karting game. Turbo Kart Racers is a fast-paced action racer where you must complete the track three times while avoiding other player's traps and getting them with your own.

HOW DO I WIN? With clever use of traps and speed boosts, you must push yourself out front and be in first position when crossing the finish line after three laps. By looking at the data on the right of the screen while playing, you can see the position you are in.

EXPERT TIPS! Familiarize yourself with the pre-made tracks, there are some shortcuts you can search out that will save you lots of time and push you into the lead. Drive through the spinning "?" blocks to obtain a random power-up. Mushroom Boosters are the best – they give you a big speed boost.

DID YOU KNOW? You can customize your helmet, your go-kart, and even your horn sound in the game. You do this by buying them in the TKR store with coins that you pick up while racing.

JOINING IN

THESE GAMES come from the PvP (Player Vs Player) server Hypixel. We have chosen this one as it's about the most child-friendly of them all, and you can join in without having to pay anything. When you start Minecraft, click "Multiplayer," then "Add Server." Name the server "Hypixel" and in the address bar below enter "hypixel.net." Click "Add Server," then when you are back at the server list screen, click "Join Server" to enter Hypixel. Walk around to find games!

BUILD BATTLE

WHAT IS IT? No swords, battling, or smashing people here – this is a timed challenge where you are asked to build something in four minutes. Everyone else is also building the same thing! At the end, you rate each other's handiwork.

HOW DO I WIN? By adding lots of detail to your build that others might not bother with. You want your build to stand out and look special. Once the four minutes building time is over, you are teleported to everybody else's plot to rate them from Super Poop to Legendary!

EXPERT TIPS! By clicking the Netherstar in your ninth Hotbar slot, you can spawn in many character heads, customized banners, particle effects, and even mobs to improve your build.

DID YOU KNOW? Players with a YouTube rank decide on the themes for builds, and you can even have teams of two, working together!

What do you think of our pyramid? Not too shabby, eh?

Let's build it!

WRESTLING RING

Perfect for multiplayer brawls with your friends!

Some say I look a bit like Stone Cold Steve Austin!

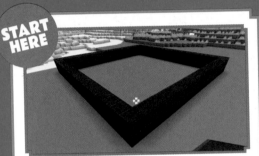

START HERE

1 GRAB YOURSELF some fluffy black wool and find a large open area. Next, lay down a row of 18 blocks next to one another. Head to the end, turn, and drop down another 18. Do this two more times to create a flat, symmetrical square, then build the walls up so they're two blocks high.

2 WITH THE base of the ring built, it's time to move on to the canvas. Traditionally, canvasses are gray, but Minecraft doesn't really have the right shade of gray, so go with white wool. For this, just cover the upper section with white wool as you won't be able to see the bottom layer.

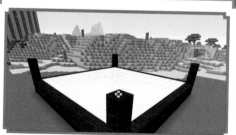

3 NEXT, PULL your black wool back out. Head to each of the four corners and build a spike on them that's three blocks tall. These are our turnbuckles, in case that wasn't clear. Turnbuckles are what wrestlers jump off. But don't do that unless you're a wrestler in real life!

4 WE HAVE two options for the ropes. The first is colored carpet, while the second is horizontal end rods. Basically, carpet has more color options, but rods look more ropelike. If you go with the carpet, you'll need to build the turnbuckles up by another single block each.

118

5 **HEAD BACK** into the Creative menu and equip some gray wool. It's steel steps–building time! Go over the top rope and to the outside. At the base of the turnbuckle, lay one block on either side. Put another block in the middle, then build it up so it resembles a diamond shape.

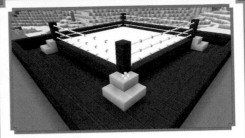

6 **WHAT'S A** wrestling ring without mats on the outside and a guard barricade? Grab some black carpet, count four blocks out from both sides of the steps, and draw an L shape. Continue the square around the outside, fill in the gaps, and build a two-block-high wall around it.

7 **PICK A** side of your wrestling ring, any side, and knock out all of that wall except for four blocks on each end. Build one side nine blocks out, make a two-block-high wall for the east side, then create a 4x4 little room on the end that connects back onto the original wall.

8 **GRAB NETHER** steps, a button, and your black wool again. In the small cubicle, the time keeper and announcer's area, lay down two steps to act as seats in front of the two walls. To the left of the chair on the right-hand side, add a block of wool with a button on top.

BUILD THIS!

Ha, ha! If you're Stone Cold, I'm The Rock!

9 **TO FINISH,** all we need now is a commentary area. For this, build two sets of 2x5 rectangles on the floor. Add steps on the backside of the second and fourth blocks. Then on the table in front of the chairs, add blocks of gray wool with paintings on to act as monitors. Ready for an epic PvP brawler battle!

HOW TO MAKE A GLADIATOR COLOSSEUM!

The name means "gigantic," and this is a BIG build. Create yourself an amphitheater fit for Gladiators!

It's a giant arena, ideal for PvP multiplayer battles!

INFO

GLADIATOR COLOSSEUM!

Difficulty:
HARD

Time needed:
3 HOURS

EXTRA INFO:
This is one gigantic build, a challenge to keep you busy!

1

LAY THE FOUNDATIONS

Getting the circular foundation right is important. To create it, grab some stone, then lay down the rows of blocks diagonally to one another in the following formation: 8, 4, 2, 1, 2, 1, 1. Turn to the right: 2, 1, 2, 4, 8. Repeat the formation until you have all four quarters connected.

2

BUILD IT UP

Once the foundation is complete, build all the walls up by three blocks so they're all four high in total. Use this as an opportunity to see whether your groundwork is level by standing in the middle and looking at the walls. If any don't match the walls opposite, something's gone wrong.

3

4

SAFETY FIRST

Grab some stone blocks and run them around the outside of the walls. Then with a fence of your choosing, cover all the stone blocks (this will act as your guardrail). After that is complete, go around the outside of the stone with yet another layer of stone.

TAKE YOUR TIME

Next, pull some stone half slabs from the creative menu and lay them around the outside of the stone blocks. Believe it or not, these half slabs are actually going to end up looking like seats in your colosseum. This next step is going to take you a while . . .

5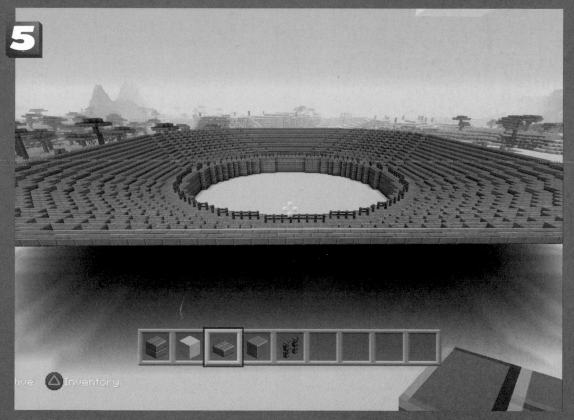

BUILD IT UP

Now we're going to repeat the last step again, only this time we're going around the half slabs one block out and up (like a step formation, almost). You'll need to do this a total of 12 more times to build up the sides of the amphitheater. What you should be left with is a kind of bowl shape, which will act as the inside of your arena. Now it's time to start building up the walls of your amphitheater.

CONNECTING COLUMNS

Pull out your stone bricks again and from behind the final row of half slabs build a column going down. Now we're going to need to turn this column into a wall surrounding the outside of the arena, so let's build more columns parallel to the outer half slabs.

ROMAN PILLARS

Pick a wall and smash a 6x6 hole to create a door frame out of chiseled quartz blocks. Lay down quartz stairs, build a five-high column out of pillar quartz, then add chiseled quartz on top. On the other sides lay more stairs, and also on both sides at the top. Connect the quartz stairs.

A STAIRWAY UP

From the center of the doorframe, count seven blocks in. With stone bricks, build a stairway up to the half slabs. Smash those out of the way. Use stone to create a platform at the end, which should connect to flat half slabs (behind the stone bricks and stone block with fences on).

A BIG ENTRANCE

On the left and right sides of the stairs, drop down some quartz pillars. Build them up so they're three blocks higher than the front half slabs. Create a roof over the top and your entrance way into the arena, for the crowd, is complete. Keep these last few steps in mind.

BUILDING A WALL

At the base of the stairs, one block diagonally away, build an eight-wide wall on both sides. Replace the middle four blocks with a light source. Underneath the light replace the stone bricks with two stone blocks and two chiseled stone blocks. Mirror this above the light source.

REPEAT ON OTHER SIDE

Next up, we're going to repeat Steps 7 through to 10, but on the opposite side of the colosseum. So: find the center of the wall, smash it, build pillars, stairs, light source walls on either side, and add an entrance. Try to get a feel for how pillars are built. There's more to come!

12

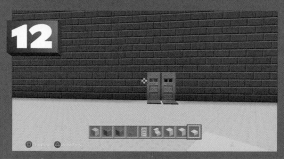

IRON DOORS

You should now be left with two outer walls in your gigantic building with nothing on them. Pick a wall, and in the center punch a 4x2 hole and fill it with iron doors. Grab some stone pressure plates and lay them in front of and behind the doors so they open easily.

13

PREPARE FOR BATTLE

On the other side of the door, build a small room out of stone bricks, and add in another door on the opposite end leading into the arena area. Drop down some pressure plates once more so the door opens. If you're going to use the arena for PvP battles, add in chests of loot now.

14

ONE MORE TIME

Run straight across the arena, smash in a door hole, and fill it with iron doors. Add pressure plates, build a small room, add chests if need be, and add a door to the back wall for entry from the outside. Once that's done, your colosseum should be starting to take shape.

15

CONNECTING UP

Head back to the outside of the arena and look for your quartz pillars. Level with where you joined up the stairs at the top of the pillars, continue that row of quartz half slabs all the way around the outside so that it eventually connects back on itself.

16

FILL IN THE WALLS

Back on the inside, by the stairs, we're going to fill in the walls. On the left and right of the light source walls, build a column that's one block out. Add another next to it, then another light source wall. Curve it around to the wall behind you, build it again where needed, and you're done.

17

BUILDING PILLARS

Now we're fixing up the outside. Add in a row of chiseled stone around the top followed by a row of quartz blocks on top of that. Add pillars on the far left and right sides of the main wall, and pillars on the smaller walls. Continue the pillars upward to level with the quartz blocks.

18

A STRONG STRUCTURE

After you've run quartz slabs all around the top of the upper pillars, head to the sides with the iron doors. Build pillars to the left and right of the doors, more pillars a few blocks away from those, and again on the smaller walls. With these last two steps, don't forget to build them again on the opposite sides.

19

BIG IS BEST!

Time to build our upper area of the gladiator arena. On every pillar, build another one sitting on top of it. After all your pillars are built, connect the tops, from step to step, with quartz half slabs. Now, above the half slabs, add quartz blocks so they run around the top.

20

IMPRESSIVE WALLS

Go to the iron doors. Past the fence and one block away from the stone rim, lay down two stone bricks with a two-block gap. Behind them add a column of bricks/stone/bricks and connect it up. Build a wall behind with pillars at each end. Add in a quartz stripe horizontally and the window area.

21

BUILD A SKYBOX

Behind the pillars, build the walls out by five blocks, then end on another stone pillar. Create the roof by adding a platform of quartz blocks surrounded by half slabs. Inside, a seat can be made out of two wooden blocks and armor stands on a platform with heads on to look like people.

22

TWO BY TWO

With one skybox complete, it's time to head on over to the opposite side and build another. Build it just like in the last step. Chiseled bricks to start, then pillars, then walls, then the roof, then the inside. Use this also as a chance to zoom out and admire your handiwork.

23

A CENTRAL PILLAR

Run blocks from the center of each entry to determine the middle of the arena, lay a four square of pillar quartz, and break away the other blocks. Build the pillars up so they're seven blocks tall. Run stairs around the bottom and upside-down stairs around the top. Half slabs go in the middle.

24

DECORATIVE QUARTZ

Back on the outside, where the quartz blocks sit on the pillars, add two more rows of quartz all the way around. To create this effect in the quartz, smash a 3x3 hole directly above the pillars then place stairs in the corners of the hole before dropping a block in the top middle with stairs.

25

OPTIONAL EXTRA

This is optional. If you prefer the sandy look of the floor inside, stick with that. If not, dig a trench from each of the doors to the pillar in the middle and lay down cobblestone. You could add two more doors on the empty walls to turn this into a four-player PvP battle map!

Let's build it!

DETECTOR RAIL ROLLER COASTER

This tricky build creates a fast-paced and thrilling roller coaster . . .

INFO

DETECTOR RAIL ROLLER COASTER

Difficulty:
HARD

It gets a bit complicated laying detector rails

Time needed:
90 MINS

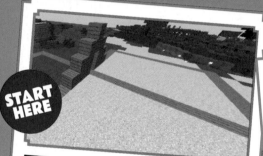

START HERE

1 **ROLLER COASTERS** are fun to build in Minecraft, and we're going to show you how to take them to the next level with detector rails. First, plan out the layout of your coaster with wood blocks; have areas that are flat and areas that go up and down to give the riders a thrill!

2 **TO ATTRACT** thrill seekers, your roller coaster has to be attractive. Add in things like a flag, vines creeping up over the wooden structures, cacti, and lakes. We want to give the impression there are mysteries to be uncovered as you ride, to make people want to line up!

3 **USING NORMAL** rails, lay out the roller coaster track on top of the wooden blocks all the way around your coaster. This will be the basic track that you can add to with more complicated rails and features later. Sadly, you can't ride it, yet, as we've not placed any powered rails.

4 **YOUR COASTER** is going nowhere until these powered rails are added. Add them on every steep part, after each corner, or wherever you want to give the riders a boost. The powered rails need power, so either place hidden redstone torches under the track, or a lever next to the track, and switch it on.

126

5 **THIS IS** the start and end of the coaster. Create a section of powered rail, with a dip, to stop the minecart so that the riders can get on and off. Place a button next to the powered rail; this will act as a starter to get the minecart going. Buttons power the rail only for a short time, unlike levers.

6 **HERE COME** the detector rails! By placing a detector rail on the track and dispensers on either side of the track, you can have the minecart trigger an event to make the coaster more exciting! dispensers are great: They will "dispense" whatever you put inside. We put fireworks in ours!

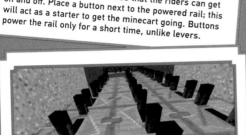

7 **THE GRAND** finale of our roller coaster is an encounter with a spitting llama! We want the minecart to pause in front of him, so that riders risk being spat at. We added a detector rail to set off redstone under the coaster with repeaters set to four ticks. Play with timings to get it just right.

8 **NEXT TO** the llama, we have built a dip in the track out of powered rails. This is the track that the redstone and repeaters are going to power. Riders get stuck with a llama staring and spitting at them and, just as they think it's going to come at them, the track is powered again and off they go!

9 **NOW THAT** you know all the secrets of powered rails and detector rails you can build roller coasters of any size and type! We continued to expand ours with a second crazy llama wearing a blue carpet, and vines growing all over our wooden blocks. Don't forget to exit through the gift shop!

BUILD THIS!

I wouldn't say I'm crazy. I just like a boogie, now and again.

Let's build it!

SWIMMING POOL

Splish, splash in this summertime build!

Ooo... I'd love to have a swim in this pool!

START HERE

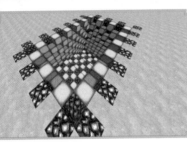

1 SWIMMING POOLS are easy – they're just holes in the ground filled with water, right? True, but making them look like real life takes a bit more creative Minecraft skill. In our example here, we have given the walls of our pool a checkerboard effect using sea lanterns, blue stained glass, and glowstone behind to shine through for effect.

2 YOU CAN make your swimming pool as big or as small as you like to complement your Minecraft world, ours is 12x7 blocks. We finished off the outside of our pool with stone slabs and quartz blocks so that is has that vacation hotel pool feel to it. You could even add some loungers!

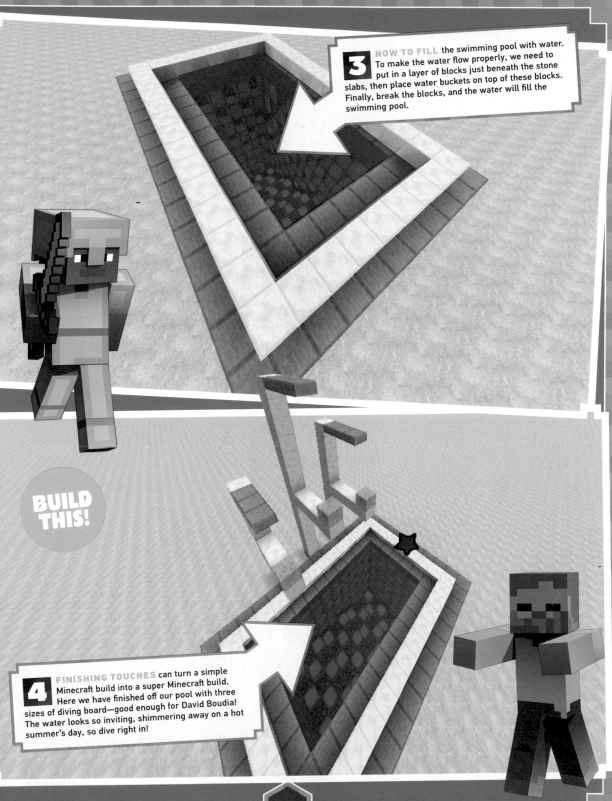

3 NOW TO FILL the swimming pool with water. To make the water flow properly, we need to put in a layer of blocks just beneath the stone slabs, then place water buckets on top of these blocks. Finally, break the blocks, and the water will fill the swimming pool.

BUILD THIS!

4 FINISHING TOUCHES can turn a simple Minecraft build into a super Minecraft build. Here we have finished off our pool with three sizes of diving board—good enough for David Boudia! The water looks so inviting, shimmering away on a hot summer's day, so dive right in!

SURVIVAL DIARY

ON THE ISLAND

The island: A decent-sized island with one big tree, a small hill, enough grass to spawn animals, and lots of sand. Perfect for your first survival challenge!

The objective: Build a luxury yacht to escape on! Those tiny little rowboats just won't do. I'll need to collect all sorts of materials to build it and get provisions for the journey.

Only I can help make your bed!

DAY 1

After spawning on the island, I look around. There's a small hill that will be perfect for a house, and a few cows to keep me company. Maybe I can treat this like a vacation! I set about chopping the tree to make a workbench and some tools. Then I quickly build a small hut. There aren't any sheep for wool, so I can't sleep. I listen to the groans of zombies smashing at my door all night and clasp on to my sword tightly just in case.

DAY 2

Thanks to the hill, there's a small space to start a mine under my house and get some stone to upgrade my tools. I also harvest the grass for seeds and start putting a small farm together for bread. One of the island's cows is sacrificed so I can have a steak dinner. Yum! It's all coming together, but during the night I get attacked by a zombie in full gold armor. There's a big fight, but I manage to win and steal his gold chestpiece. Score!

DAY 4

There's a thunderstorm during the night, and the island becomes infested with skeletons. I have to fight a clear path to the mine, avoiding the spider jockey. He's far too tough for me. I descend even further into the earth in hunt of some coal, but can't find any. I haven't even found a cave yet! I return to the surface to trim my trees for wood to build the boat and plant some new ones.

Islands aren't big enough!

DAY 7

After a few days I have a small forest going, and it's time to start making my boat. It needs to be big enough to survive a month at sea, with enough room to live in. I also need to make sure I have lots of food to survive the journey. So far I've been getting good at surviving, but now I need to kick it up a notch!

DAY 10

After collecting loads of oak planks, I finally start building the hull of the boat and a pier to set off from. It's a horrible rainy day, though, so all of the island zombies are still alive. I have to dodge one going for a swim while I finish building the base.

DAY 12

The building and farming is going well, but it's starting to get really lonely on this island by myself. I need to make some friends! Since all of the zombies and skeletons only seem to want to eat me, they're out of the picture. I try to befriend the island pig, but he isn't interested in the only thing I have—wheat. Thankfully, two cows come running, so I quickly fence them in and force them to be my friends forever and ever and ever. Some extra friends also happen to fall into the pen. Score!

DAY 14

The boat is coming along nicely. I've built a hut for steering the boat and a living quarters below deck. I've even got a storage area to put my provisions in. I have some bread, but not quite enough to set sail yet. I also need to find wool to make a sail, but there aren't any sheep on my island. My only hope is that one will appear in the night one day.

I'll come knocking on your door!

DAY 15

There's an accident in the pen I lock all of my "friends" in. While saying hello to them, I attract a creeper. I try to run away, but it explodes right by the pen, blowing up all of my animal pals in the process. I cry for 10 minutes, but then I realize I now have enough cooked beef and pork to take on my journey at sea! Their sacrifice won't be in vain.

DAY 18

A sheep finally appears on the island. I'm saved! I run down to the mines to find iron for to craft shears. Then I wait. I snip its wool away and then watch and wait until it regrows so I can snip it again. With only one sheep on the entire island, this might take a while.

You can't run away from me!

DAY 20

After two days of watching the sheep, I've finally got enough wool to make a sail. I'm finally ready to leave the island! I pack all of the food on board, drop the sail, and head off into the sunset. It's been a long three weeks on the tiny island, but I'd definitely do it all over again. It's such a good Minecraft challenge!

Make friends, not bacon!

MINECRAFT
GLIDE MINI GAME
Top tips on gliding your way around tight corners!

You can play Glide, Battle, and Tumble on console Minecraft!

THE NEED FOR SPEED

Winning in *Glide* is all about speed! You're dropped in the deep end, competing against friends or players around the world. There is a Time Attack Mode where the objective is to get to the finish line before your competitors, and Score Attack Mode where you must fly through the green rings to earn three points—highest score wins! Flying through arrow gates will give you a speed burst.

PICK A MAP

There are four maps you can select from in *Glide*. You start off in Cavern, which is a twisting track through rocky outcrops, Yeti is loads of fun with a giant beast peeking out from icy glaciers, the Kraken map whizzes you past pirate ships where a sea beast awaits, and Dragon gives you a preview of the Chinese Mythology Resource Pack, as you fly past dragons. Each one needs lightning reflexes if you are to stand any chance of winning—take a few goes to learn the route by playing solo before joining multiplayer.

REACH FOR THE SKIES

Successfully racing around each map will rely on you being at the correct height for important twists and turns. Keep an eye open for the fiery square pools with steam coming off them. This steam will push you up in the air, giving you new height that you can use to survey the area before swooping down.

REAR VIEW MIRROR

Want to find out who is on your tail? The "Look Behind" button will give you a glimpse, useful in Time Attack Mode. If they are following you because you know where you're going and they don't, lead them toward a trap! A cliff face will do, just dart to the side at the last minute and laugh as they splat into the rocks. It's also useful to look behind on the finish line if you're in first place – there might be someone coming up fast!

CUT THE CORNER

Still not managing to win? We bet you're missing out on all the shortcuts that have been hidden away throughout the maps. A good plan would be to spend some time playing the game in solo mode again where you can go slowly and explore the walls and hidden areas to familiarize yourself with the shortcuts. Some are really tiny gaps and you will need to be highly accurate to make it through without bashing your head!

MINECRAFT
BATTLE MINI GAME
The winner is the last one standing, can you survive?

BEAT THAT CHEST

Battle is a kind of Hunger Games where you've got to attack anyone and everyone you come across. Be sure to check out the contents of every chest you discover – they will have armor, food, weapons, and potions to help you.

POTION POWER

There are negative and positive potions. In one-on-one combat, you will gain a big advantage if you throw a negative potion at a foe, giving more damage than a sword swipe alone. Also, munch some apples to increase your hunger bar.

CROWDED BATTLES

Up to 16 players can now battle it out simultaneously in *Battle*, which makes for some frantic games! The maps don't get any bigger, and there are no extra chests, so when you are all facing off against each other at the start, jump into the chests if you are confident of getting there before someone else. Or a good tactic is just to run away in the opposite direction! Chests refill over time, so you can always come back later. Pushing people from a high height is an effective way of causing damage. If you see someone falling from a height, a few swipes with a weapon could just finish them off.

GRAB THEIR STUFF!

When you manage to kill someone, they will drop all of their stuff, which is then ripe for the picking! To start with, you need to concentrate on defending yourself, keeping out of the way of other players while you stock up on essential armor, weapons, potions, and food. Once you are confident you have some great stuff in your inventory, you can then go on the hunt – taking players out with a clever combination of throwing potions and attacking, while wearing some good armor.

MINECRAFT
CONSOLE EDITION
TUMBLE MINI GAME

Shovels or snowballs – time for some Tumble!

DIG FOR VICTORY

There are two styles of gameplay in *Tumble*, one where everyone has a shovel and must dig the blocks from underneath enemies. The other is snowballs, which we will discuss in a bit. Shovels is certainly the toughest mode, as it is close-up gameplay. One important thing to avoid is soul sand. These brown blocks will slow you down, making you an easy target! If you spot two players having a bit of a fight, creep up behind one of them and dig the block underneath them away before they know you're even there!

ICY MOVES

You need to use slightly different tactics to win in a Snowball game. These icy weapons can be used close-up or from a distance and the trick is to aim at the other player's feet, trying to smash the block they are just about to walk on to. The snowballs are unlimited and fly through the air in an arc, so aim higher than the enemy to knock them off a ledge. A great tactic is to climb up to the top layers in the map, make a hole in the ground, and fire hundreds of snowballs through the hole at the players below!

SKIN PACK FUN

THE MINI GAME MASTERS SKIN PACK was released to celebrate *Glide* going live on PS4 and Xbox One. It's full of super sporting skins that look great when you're gliding around the tricky maps in *Glide*, battling for your life in Battle, or tumbling off ledges in *Tumble*. The skins are split into teams—Team Creeper, Team Guardian, and Team Zombie to name just a few, with all kinds of weird combinations going on (chicken on the head, anyone?). You can sample some of these skins for free, but the full pack will need to be purchased.

TRICKY TROPHIES

There are trophies you can achieve if you complete set challenges in the game. You get a "S-No Throw" if you win a game without throwing a single snowball. To get this, run around avoiding other players while they battle it out with each other, then knock the blocks from underneath the final enemy with your fists. Attack that player with 25 snowballs in a single round and you will get "Snow Storm." We also got a "Hotshot" trophy for landing a snowball on someone while we fell into the lava!

SPECTATOR SPORT

In both *Battle* and *Tumble*, once you die, you turn into a bat and can fly around the map checking out all the cool stuff. This is a great way of familiarizing yourself with the various types of terrain before you jump back into another game. In such fast and frantic mini-games, taking your time as a bat can be a welcome break!

Let's build it!

THE MEGA MEAT MACHINE!

Wait a minute . . . I don't like the sound of this build!

Your favorite meat at the touch of a button!

START HERE

Gather this stuff!

 1 **FEELING HUNGRY?** This hard build project is a Mega Meat Machine! We're showing you how to make a vending machine for meat using tricky redstone. First of all make a 7x3x1 box out of the block of your choice, then knock three holes in it and fill with a contrasting block, with three buttons on top.

2 **ON THE** back of your vending machine box, put three redstone torches on the three contrasting blocks. Now you need to dig a giant hole underneath this mega machine for all the redstone circuits we're going to add later. It should be 7x5 and two blocks deep.

3 **PLACE THREE** wool blocks behind the machine, up against the outer wall, with one-block gaps between them. On top of these, place three hoppers for each wool block, but crouch while placing them so they lead into the block below them. Place a chest on top of each hopper stack.

4 **BREAK TWO** of the wool blocks, leaving the farthest right one. Now place a hopper while looking at the side of the wool block, then a farther three hoppers leading into the first one, but place these while crouching, otherwise you will open the hopper, not place it leading into the next one.

5 **NOW GO** to the front of the machine. You need to place a dropper facing up in the center of the wall, then place six more hoppers leading into the dropper, for the final one you will have to break the remaining wool block. Remember—you need to be crouching while placing them for this to work.

6 **TIME TO** get those Wool blocks back out again! Place one next to the dropper, one in the corner created by the hoppers, and the final one, one block away from the dropper (as you can see in the picture above). These will be used for taking redstone signals around your machine!

7 **HERE COMES** the complicated part! Place a comparator (it looks like a triangle!) between the dropper and the wool block, facing into the wool block. Place two repeaters, one facing into the wool block next to the dropper, the other one facing out from the wool block in the corner next to the hoppers.

8 **TIME FOR** some redstone fun! Place two redstone dust on the ground—one next to each repeater. Then a third behind the wool block, as shown above. With that done, fill the three chests placed earlier with three types of your favorite meat — one type of meat in each chest. Mmm . . . pork chops.

BUILD THIS!

Meat Machine!

Wow! I Think every shop should have a meat machine!

9 **YOU NOW** must fill in the hole in front of your machine to hide the mechanics, but be sure not to click any of the redstone while you do as your machine will break down! On the front, place three item frames with your meat choices in each frame to show people which button to press. Now, pressing a button delivers some meat!

INFO

MUSHROOM KINDGOM
Difficulty:
MEDIUM
Time needed:
5 HOURS
EXTRA INFO:
Why not imagine who lives in your mushroom kingdom!

HOW TO MAKE A MUSHROOM KINGDOM

No, it's not Mario's kingdom, but it's pretty close!

There's not mush-room with all these toadstools about!

Creating your very own colorful fairyland to play around in requires plenty of unique imagination, but here are a few ideas from us on how to craft your very own toadstool-and-mushroom-festooned magical place!

HOW TO MAKE A MUSHROOM KINGDOM

NUKE IT!

We need to find a nice flat area and then nuke it with TNT! What you'll want to end up with is a 17x17 square hole that's around seven blocks deep. You'll be using TNT to do most of the work, don't worry about it being perfect. We'll clear it up later.

MAKE A CHANNEL

Next, pull out the white mushroom block and find the rough middle of the hole. Now go ahead and create a 6x6 square. Now you're good to build the walls up high enough so they tower over the rest of the world – but don't hit the clouds.

BASE TOWER

Now it's time to add some shaping to the rectangle, which we'll be calling the base tower. Using mushroom, draw some diagonal lines in any formation heading up each of the sides.

Next, build up from the ground to meet the lines. With four of these done, now you'll need to start adding some random shapes to decorate them. Next, we'll start to build the roof.

UNDER MY ROOF

Count seven blocks down from the top. Work out where the middle of each side is, and mark the middle two blocks with mushrooms. Now build each

17 blocks from the base tower. From the end of the arms, build and join the four-long sections of what will be our red dome.

THE DOME

Build up each of the four 4-wide arms so they stand six blocks tall. Then add five blocks behind, then four, three, two, and two sets of one. You should now be able to connect the four sections across the top. Now just build up the other sections the same way.

LOOK UNDERNEATH

On the underside of the giant mushroom, build a one-high rim on the inside, then a two-high rim behind that, and fill in the ceiling. Go back to the red top and smash out sections at random and then replace with white wool.

7

LIGHT-UP TIME

With the top finished, your stem will now be bathed in darkness. To fix this, just grab end rods and run them from the ceiling and along the stem, then place a sea lantern at the bottom. Now you'll be able to see what's what!

8

WIN THE POOLS

Check to make sure the distances from stem to wall are all the same, then use polished diorite to create the pool. Add sea lanterns, then fill up. Now go around and find the center of each of the four walls and knock out a few blocks to mark them.

9

FILL HER UP

Use dirt blocks to make the floor level with the pool area. Run dark oak fence around outside. Now go back to middle of each wall, and create four sets of 5-wide steps leading all the way back up to ground level, and add torches.

THE LEGO KINGDOM

LEGO HAS already beaten you to it! LEGO set 21129 is a Minecraft Mushroom Island, complete with a giant red-and-white mushroom and mooshroom roaming around causing trouble.

WHILE IT'S easy to build these LEGO Minecraft sets, the fun is in playing with the characters and locations once you've built it.

YOU'VE GOTTA love the LEGO Minecraft creepers and mooshroom! LEGO don't often make new pieces, preferring to use the millions they already have made, but the creeper legs are unique!

10

LEAFY STUFF

Grab a leaf block and create four 3-wide, 3-high hedges on both sides of all steps. Now connect them in a diagonal fashion. With polished diorite, create the step/leaf combo one block higher than the steps on the left and right of the main steps.

11

GARDENING TODAY

From behind the diorite lay down grass blocks, then add one block up and behind until you have four rows, including the row level with the diorite. Run diorite up the sides and connect around the back top. Add flowers to your heart's content!

12

FIRST HOUSE

Make an 11x7 rectangle. At the back, lay down a 5x5 square for the rear. Build all corners up by four blocks, add in doorway, then a front wall and connect white mushroom along the top. Fill walls with dirt, then add front and back roofs.

13

HOLY SHROOMS!

Do mushroom people have churches? Well, they do now! Start with the door frame, add two rows above, then place in the poking-out parts on the sides. Now mirror the bottom, only above. Lay down the mushrooms on top in a step formation.

14

CHURCH HALL

Below this mushroom staircase, you should be able to create walls leading downward. Create the back section while taking note of the shape of the structure, and fill in the windows and add a mini roof at the back. Your fungi church is done!

15

BLACKSMITH FORGE

Start with your three quartz steps, then place blocks behind either side with fence on. Build fence up by three, then place blocks on top. Build out so the front is 10 blocks long. Add the room on the left, and the forge area on the right.

ACACIA AVENUE

Can you see how all the trees look out of place? Don't worry, we're going to rebuild them out of our two mushroom blocks. Acacia trees work the best here due to their natural shape, but any tree will do. Experiment with what you have on hand!

MUSHROOM FOR ALL!

Now just hack away the leaves on top of the tree and replace with red mushroom, then chop down the wooden trunk section, and change it to white mushroom. You've completed this build! Invite all your friends around for a quorn feast!

This is the place to be if you're . . . a fun guy!

INFO

SURVIVAL FARM

Difficulty:
EASY

Time needed:
1 HOUR

EXTRA INFO:
You can mix up the instructions to make the farm to suit you. Put in what will scare them most!

BUILD A SURVIVAL FARM

Tackling Survival Mode can be made easier with a well-stocked farm. Let us show you how to build one . . .

PLANNING THE BARN

We need to build the floor plan for our large farm barn. Grab some spruce logs and drop four down with two blocks of space in between. Add two more rows, two blocks apart, north of the previous row. On the far right, count four blocks out and place a row of three blocks, two apart. Build the wood up by four blocks except for the middle-left three, which are three blocks high. Fill in the left, right, and top sides with three-high stone blocks.

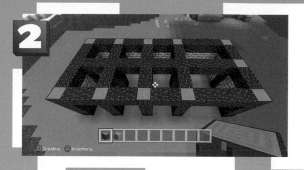

RAISE THE ROOF

Next we're going to build the base of our roof. Grab your spruce logs once more and fill in the left and right sides. From here, run a line across the middle, going directly on top of the shorter pillars we laid down in the last step. Run two more rows on the north and south sides, then finish up by running three more smaller rows from south to north and you're done.

WALKING THE PLANK

Add some spruce planks and a wooden fence to your hotbar. Ignoring the large gap to the right, run the spruce planks along the ground from left to right. When you reach the large gap, turn and enter the structure and drop some more planks as well as a gate so you have easy access. Now place the fences on top of the planks to make sure that any horses you wrangle don't escape and run amok!

UP ON THE ROOF

Up next, the roof of our stable. For this, head back to the top with your spruce planks and wherever you see the white side of the spruce logs, place a plank. Create a step effect by building one block out, laying a block on top, then deleting the corner of the L shape. Do this on both sides until you eventually meet the natural middle, which will end up being the main strip of the roof.

SPRUCE IT UP

Your roof won't look much like a roof at this point, but that's okay. Here's a tip to make a roof less dull. Grab some steps, spruce steps to be exact. In between each of the planks, lay down the steps and connect them to the next plank along. Repeat this process until all the gaps are covered in steps, then run half slabs round the bottom and fill in the west and east sides with spruce to finish off your lovely roof.

6

BUILDING THE BARN

With your stable finished, find a large plot of land nearby for your barn. Ours is to the right of the stable, but feel free to change this as you see fit. Next, with spruce logs, drop down a row of five blocks, count five blocks to the right, and add in another row of five spruce logs. On each row, build the sides up by five, then place a 3x3 wall of stone blocks in the middle. Round it out by placing a row of spruce logs on top.

PUT UP A SPIKE

Build a five-high spike on top of the center of the arch. To the left and right of the spike, put two more sets of planks in a step formation. When that's completed, grab your trusty spruce logs and while looking down, place blocks on top of the plank steps. If you've done this correctly, you shouldn't need to place a middle block in the top center as it'll already be there.

7

ONE BIG LOG

On each of the corners and the tops, add a single spruce log to create the effect that it's all one big long log that's been lowered into place. Head to the middle and on the left and right build up by three, then connect the two spikes to create an entrance arch. Add more single blocks for the log effect and end by placing spruce planks in a step formation on each side.

8

9

MAKING THE WALLS

For the walls, build from the back of the barn to the front. To ensure the wood is all facing the same way, build it from ground level upward (laying them down from left to right means the wall will take on a different shape thanks to the way wood placement works). Build walls on both sides and be sure to extend them by 12 blocks. Don't worry about the solid wood look as we'll be sprucing it up later.

AND REPEAT

For this next part, we're going to need to rebuild the front side once more, only on the opposite end. You can either head back to Step 6 and repeat the instructions or if you're up for a challenge, create the back by copying the front from memory! The general rule here is to lay down spruce logs as your guideline, then add in the stone bricks and the step planks afterward.

10

SPRUCE STEPS

Next we'll be putting what we learned from Step 5 back into action again. Pick a wall, then count two blocks in from the left and drop in a spruce log facing up. Count another two blocks along and drop down two spruce logs next to one another. Count two blocks again, then drop another one down. Create a step effect heading into the middle out of spruce logs to create the frame of our roof.

STONE SIDES

For this next part, fill in all the spaces, from left to right, between the spruce frame with spruce steps. Once that's done, your barn roof should be fully completed, so now we'll tackle the sides of the barn. If you're after something quick and simple, then just grab some stone, and then mine up four rows and the centerpiece before filling them in with stone. There you go, nice and easy.

HOMES FOR ANIMALS

For the inside of the barn, connect the two sections parallel with the front where the logs stick out. Count three blocks along and build a spruce pillar, then four blocks and another pillar, then three. In the gaps lay down spruce planks with fences on top of them to create three animal pens. Mirror this on the opposite side, then you can add torches to make sure you don't get any uninvited guests during the night.

Can't wait to see our new home!

YOUR FIVE A DAY

What's a farm without a decent supply of crops for your adventuring? To finish this build, build six 5x5 plots and dig up a one-block moat around all of them. Grab yourself a water bucket and fill the moat; this will help your crops grow much more quickly. Add fencing around the entire area, gates to get in and out, and a single block of grass between each section for access. Now that this is finished, go out and find some animals!

L1 IS YOUR FRIEND

When playing Battle Mode on Playstation, speed is everything. When you're fighting over the same chests it's important to be as fast as possible. Try to take everything from a chest at once instead of picking each item up.

lauser717 has left the game.

Previous   Next

BATTLE MINI GAME TIPS!

Learn to fight like a pro with these hints . . .

LEARN THE MAP

There are only three maps at the moment, each one with chests hidden around them. Learning exactly where these are, so you can take the quickest route to them, will give you a boost over the competition.

Invulnerability has worn off. Fight!

Previous   Next

BUDDY UP

If you're playing with a friend, teaming up to share your resources is a great way to stop enemies taking you by surprise. You will have to fight each other at the end, though.

RUN AWAY!

Simple, right? Although picking the right direction is important. If you want to survive, you'll have to run in the exact opposite direction to everyone else.

HAVE SNACKS

Your hunger can drop quite quickly, so getting food from chests is important. Make sure you're never hungry so your health can always fill up.

THE SLIME BLOCK RAILWAY!

Forget Thomas . . . the future is Slime Block Railways! Here's our step-by-step mega-build . . .

INFO

SLIME BLOCK RAILWAY

Difficulty:
HARD
YOU NEED TO FOLLOW CLOSELY TO GET YOUR SLIME WORKING.

Time needed:
1 HOUR

EXTRA INFO:
Good training in how to combine slime, nether, and redstone.

There's so much fun to be had in Minecraft building railways, minecarts, roller coasters, and other cool machines. Have you tried combining the impressive might of slime blocks, nether bricks, and redstone, though? In this mega-build, we're going to show you how to build an impressive railway station and train first, then how to fire up your engine with slime blocks and watch it go! You can take the techniques you learn here and use them to create some impressive machines to show off to your friends. So, let's start with Step 1 . . .

Stick with me and I'll show you how to make a railway!

152

1

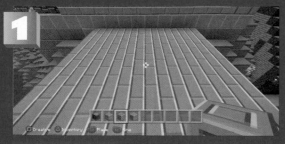

FIND A SPACE

Let's begin by finding a gigantic open space, preferably the side of a mountain with nothing opposite, giving plenty of room for building. From here, build a platform that's seven blocks out of the mountain and eight blocks across. Next, fill your hotbar with spruce wood, stone bricks, chiseled stone bricks, and stone.

2

MAKE A PLATFORM

Build two rows of chiseled stone bricks on the left and right side of the platform 33 blocks long. Then from the left, count one block, and on the second block, drop in a row of stone also 33 blocks long. Head to the right side and do it again. Grab your spruce wood and place horizontal rows with a gap between each section.

3

COLUMNS

Once your railway line is complete, head back to the start. On the right where the chiseled stone brick starts, add two more chiseled bricks to the outside. On this 2x2 section, build each corner up 11 high. Back on the chiseled row, count one block out and with a cobblestone wall, place 10 of them on top of each other.

4

TIME FOR A BRIDGE

Count a block out and build a spike that's nine high. Miss a gap and build one eight high. Do this until you get to a four-high spike, then add another four-high spike one block away from it. Repeat the process, only in reverse until you're back up to a second 10-high cobblestone wall. The walls should look symmetrical.

5

TOWER OF POWER

Right off the last spike, build a 2x2 tower 11 high. For a bridge, grab stone brick slabs and place them on top of all of your spikes, and fill in the gaps with slabs half a block higher. Delete the right side of the chiseled brick row at the bottom and replace it with stone half-slabs so the railway line slightly pokes out.

6

DOWN TO GROUND

Back at the first 2x2 tower, build it down to ground or water level. At the base of the tower, cover the outside in a 4x4 square. Now build another 4x4 square on top of that. Place stone brick steps going around the top of the square. Head to the top of the tower, add another four stone steps, and this is complete.

153

COMPLETE THE BRIDGE

Head to the other tower and repeat the step six instructions to finish it up. You'll also now need to create another two towers on the left chiseled stone brick row opposite your already complete towers and add in some spikes and half-slabs.

BUILD A STATION

Time to build a foundation. At the end of the tracks, on the far left side, build with bricks: three out, four left, six down, four left, 14 down, four right, six down, four right. On the right side, build it in reverse: three out, four right, six down, four right, 14 down, four left, six down, four left.

EXTEND THE TRACKS

Once the shape is complete, extend the railway tracks so they meet the end of the shape. Now, back to the brick shape. Build its walls two high. On every corner build a three-high wall. To finish, grab iron bars and fill in the gaps between the corners. Leave the longest sides empty.

TICKETS PLEASE

On each side of the tracks, add coal blocks. Fill in the floor area with stone blocks. In the gaps we didn't fill in, build a four-high door frame out of quartz blocks and quartz half-slabs. Around the left side of the door, build a wall out of bricks, glass panes, and quartz half-slabs for a booth.

LIGHTS, ACTION!

Head to the outside of the booth and build walls, a floor, and four more booths on the inside. Then, add a carpet on the floor. Build the walls four out, then create a box shape to turn our ticket booths into a cube structure. Add sea lanterns into the ceiling to create some light.

ROOF & STEPS

Add quartz half-slabs around the roof and you're done. You may want to add steps if your booth is floating. Head back to the opposite doorframe and add a three-high brick wall with quartz half-slabs on the top to match the doorframe. Add steps on the other side.

13

THE SLIME BLOCK TRAIN

Fill your hotbar with black wool, a slime block, a redstone block, a piston, a sticky piston, nether brick fence, and nether brick stairs. At the start of the track, place two blocks one block apart. Place black wool then three slime blocks on top. Delete the first two blocks you placed.

14

FUN WITH FUNNELS

Add two more slime on the left and right, then one block behind each. Behind the middle slime, add a piston. On the other side, place a sticky piston facing the back of the train, then in front of that, a piston facing out. Drop three slime off the piston and a nether brick fence on the last block.

15

ALL ABOARD

Add one slime block under the first and third of the new row you placed. On both sides of these blocks, add black wool to look like wheels. Grab your nether brick stairs and place one on the base of the front of the train. To power this awesome beast, drop a redstone block on the back half of the front and another one more at the back. Now all that's left to do is place a redstone block to the left of the sticky piston, delete it, and your train should chug along your track. Great work!

INSPIRATION

NORFOLK SOUTHERN The CraftyFoxe team will show you how to build this EMD GP38-2 diesel-electric locomotive step by step on YouTube.

RAILS OF WAR This is a mod created by Naiten that adds tracks, stream trains, wide turns, and everything locomotive. A dream for all trainspotters!

TRAINS IN GREENFIELD The Minecraft Transp Co has an entire server dedicated to trains and railways of all kinds. Google it for more info!

Let's build it!

SANTA'S SLEIGH

Build Santa's sleigh and reindeer in time for Xmas!

START HERE

1 **PLACE FENCEPOSTS** two-high and three blocks apart, then five gates behind each. This is the ski part of the sled. Now make the sled from red clay or wool with trapdoors for doors.

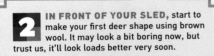

2 **IN FRONT OF YOUR SLED,** start to make your first deer shape using brown wool. It may look a bit boring now, but trust us, it'll look loads better very soon.

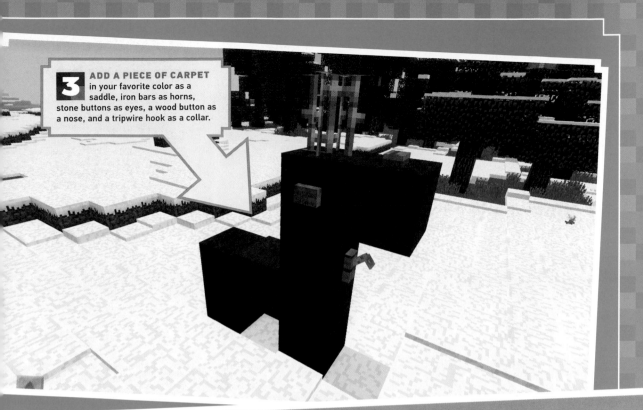

3 **ADD A PIECE OF CARPET** in your favorite color as a saddle, iron bars as horns, stone buttons as eyes, a wood button as a nose, and a tripwire hook as a collar.

4 **NOW REPEAT** the deer design eight times, with three blocks between them in the middle and two in front to get the full Santa's sleigh effect!

SANTA'S GROTTO

Prepare for a Merry Minecraft Christmas with this festive build . . .

INFO

SANTA'S GROTTO

Difficulty:
MEDIUM-HARD

Time needed:
4 HOURS

EXTRA INFO:
Build yourself
some reindeer
for extra fun!

1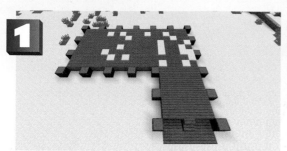

SNOW DAY

Find yourself a frosty biome and lay down a spruce wood plank floor in an L shape. It's 8x17 with the front bit being 5x6. Place spruce wood around the edge with a two-block gap in between.

2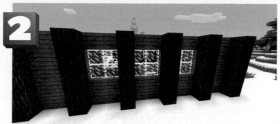

FIRST FLOOR

Build it all four blocks high on top of your floor layer. Make room for 2x2 windows where you have gaps between the spruce wood pillars. Place more spruce wood to build up your pillars.

3

GOING UP

Place slabs to act as your second floor. Put some upside-down stairs above your windows, so your second floor sticks out a bit. Place spruce wood on top all the way round.

4

SMALL ROOF

The smaller part of your L shape is just your entrance way and won't get a proper floor, so use dark oak plank stairs to make a roof on that part. Make it stick out at the front by one block.

INSPIRATION

IN ARENDSOOGG'S

Christmas Town, Santa even pays a festive visit! Ho ho ho, etc!

SANTA'S CHRISTMAS

workshop seems set up for business. Nice one EdiBoy21!

CHRISTMAS VILLAGE

by Huskii looks like it's made from gingerbread and candy!

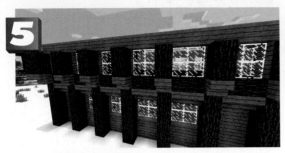

5 SECOND FLOOR

Put upside-down stairs on all of your pillars, then place spruce wood going up again to extend them for the second floor. Put 2x2 windows in the gaps like on the first floor and build your walls up.

6 BIG ROOF

Use dark oak stairs going up to a peak in the middle with slabs for the very top. Start at the layer just above the windows. Fill in the gaps where the small roof joins to the big one.

7 OPEN ENDS

It's time to fill in the empty space. Put upside-down stairs above the windows, and normal stairs at the top of your pillars. Add in another 2x2 window and fill in the rest with spruce planks.

8 FINAL TOUCHES

The main building just needs a few small final touches. Try adding a porch your front door area, and maybe a stone chimney to the side of the main building. Make sure all of your pillars are neat.

9 CANDY CANE LANE

Create a path leading up to your grotto with stone brick blocks hidden underneath the snow. Build candy canes made out of white and red clay. They're five tall, then two across and one down.

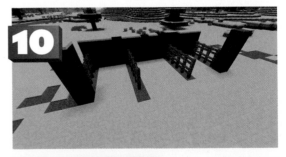

10 REINDEER STABLES

Now for your reindeer house! Make a three-high wall of spruce for the back. Then leave a gap of four blocks and place two pillars of four high at each end. Place spruce fence walls two blocks high to make pens.

SLANTED ROOF

To make the slope of the roof, use thin slabs on top of the back wall and one block behind. Go up one space for the next two rows, and then one space again for the last two. Put gates on your fence pens.

LIVESTOCK

Now we just need some reindeer to live in the pens! First, create a fenced area that connects to the grotto for them to live in. Then build your deer out of brown wool, steel fence, and buttons.

ICE AS NICE

What does Santa do when he wants to relax? He skates! Build an ice rink to the right of the grotto by digging a one-block-deep hole and placing ice over the top. Put sea lanterns underneath to light it.

INSPIRATION

STARGO123 PUT

together this snowy Christmas Surprise just in time for Santa!

CHRISTMAS VALLEY

from Team Surface looks like the most festive place on earth!

LOOK AT

all the nice presents to unwrap in Chomp2's ace holiday homestead!

IT'S CHRISTMAS!

Put a Christmas tree at the front of the grotto. Use carpet as a mat in an almost-round shape with a spruce wood trunk in the middle and build up. Decorate with wool, and a glowstone star on top.

THE ULTIMATE GUIDE TO THE END

Everything you need to know about reaching the End, fighting the Ender Dragon, and finding End cities!

All Endermen are named Gregory, you know!

Now that the End is in Pocket Edition and expanded on consoles there's suddenly a whole lot more exploring for you to do! The End can be a tricky, scary place, sometimes filled with Endermen and lots of purple, but don't worry, we've put together a guide that covers everything. We'll show you how to make a portal to get there, how to beat the Ender Dragon, and how to find End cities too!

1 ENDERMEN

Learning to fight these guys in the Overworld will help you in the End. They'll leave you alone if you don't look at them, but you'll need to fight them to get lots of ender pearls. They're fast and hard to fight, so make sure you have good armor and weapons. A good strategy is to make a two-block high base, lure them nearby, and then hit their legs. They're three blocks tall so they can't get in.

2 ENDER PEARLS

You'll need lots of ender pearls to get to the End. You can get them by farming Endermen, but they also appear in some chests in strongholds. You can also turn them into eyes of ender by adding blaze powder at a crafting table. If you make an eye of ender, you can throw it, and it'll help you find a stronghold with an end portal in it.

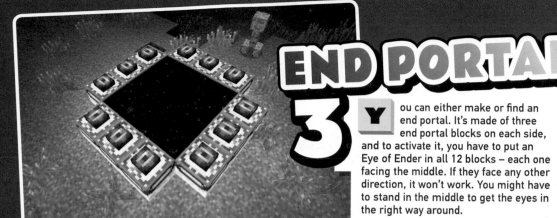

END PORTAL

3

You can either make or find an end portal. It's made of three end portal blocks on each side, and to activate it, you have to put an Eye of Ender in all 12 blocks – each one facing the middle. If they face any other direction, it won't work. You might have to stand in the middle to get the eyes in the right way around.

> Shhh . . . I'm creeping up on Steve!

Always bring a bow with you as creepers will explode if they come close to you, but a bow will keep them away

> What? There's a creeper behind me you say?!

4 PREPPING FOR BATTLE

There's a lot you need to do before you go through that portal! You can only leave if you beat the Ender Dragon or die, so you need to be well prepped before you venture out. You'll need a diamond sword, pickaxe and armor, as well as a bow and plenty of health potions. A pumpkin for your head will also help, and if you can, team up with friends and work together to beat it. It's much easier than fighting alone!

5 FIGHTING IN THE END

Fighting the Ender Dragon is just one part of the End. There are lots of other dangers to face while fighting! The End is filled with Endermen—so many that it's hard not to catch their attention. Wearing a pumpkin head can help, but it makes it hard to see the dragon. You might also spawn underground, so you'll have to reach the surface first.

Gregory Enderman, at your service.

Bows will be no use here in the End, the Endermen will teleport away before your arrows can poke them!

6 ENDER CRYSTALS

Before you start fighting the Ender Dragon properly, you'll want to destroy all of the ender crystals that heal it first. The best method is to shoot them with your bow, but you'll have to climb the pillars of the ones protected by iron bars to destroy those before hitting the crystal. If you destroy a crystal while a dragon is charging from it, you'll do a big chunk of damage at once.

7 KILLING THE DRAGON

Wow! This guide to the End is really *dragon on*!

Because it flies around, the Ender Dragon is really hard to hit. It's better to wait until it tries charging at you and then hit it in the head with a charged arrow, then quickly dodge its attack. You might be able to get a second hit in when it recoils. Hitting its head does more damage than hitting its body.

8 GATEWAY PORTALS

After you kill the dragon, a fountain will spawn in the middle that takes you back to the Overworld, but make sure you look around first! A gateway portal will also spawn, sometimes you'll find it in the sky. If you throw an ender pearl in it, it will teleport you to an island in the End. You can spawn more portals by beating the dragon again. Every time you beat it, another portal will spawn.

What am I doing here? A new place to explore!

END 9 CITIES

If you get lucky, you might find an End city on the island you teleport to through the gateway portal. They're full of chests filled with enchanted weapons and other goodies, but also danger. Instead of stairs you might have to do some clever jumping to go up the floors in the city. You'll also have to look out for enemies.

10 SHULKERS

They might look like purple blocks with cute faces, but shulkers can be really dangerous! They live in End cities and shoot out projectiles that follow you around the room and make you levitate. You have to hit or block them to get rid of them— dodging doesn't work. They have really good defense, so you need to hit them when they look out of their shells. They can drop shulker shells, which can be used to make shulker boxes for storage.

Once you've killed a shulker, be sure to pick up its shell as you can use it like a backpack and even color it to your taste!

11 END SHIPS

These are ships that are sometimes found floating near End cities if you're lucky. You'll have to build a bridge to reach one, and once inside, you'll have to beat the shulkers, but it's worth it. Inside are at least two treasure chests and an item frame containing a pair of elytra wings. They're super-rare to find, though!

Make sure you've got loads of ender pearls before you get here – you can teleport to hard-to-reach places

I can see my house from up here!

12 ELYTRA

The best item in the entire game! Elytra wings are placed in your chest armor slot and let you glide around the world. You activate them by hitting "Jump" while falling and they'll let you glide around like a bird. They make getting around the End and the Overworld a lot easier.

MINECRAFT GLOSSARY

From Armor to Weapons, here's our handy guide to Minecraft terms!

Minecraft may have been around for almost a decade at this point, but the game has grown immensely compared to what it once was. If you're completely new to the biggest game this century however, this Minecraft Glossary will help you to understand the terms in the game so you can become an intrepid explorer and champion in the cubic world in no time!

ARMOR

Getting yourself protected is one of the first things that you'll need to do in Minecraft. Leather or iron armor is attainable early on, but not so good against tougher foes. Once you have a full set of diamond armor, however, you'll be ready to take on the world.

BASE

Your base is the place you call home. While some players like to build a house, the freedom of Minecraft means that you can make it pretty much anywhere! Your base could be in the side of a mountain, underground in a cave, or even up in the treetops!

BIOME

Each distinct region of the Minecraft overworld is called a biome. For example, you may spawn in a forest full of trees, but after exploring, you may find a desert, ocean, plains, or something else. There are 40 unique biomes to discover in total.

BLOCKS

You may have noticed that Minecraft is made up of blocks – and there's a lot of them! From stone and dirt to prismarine and mossy cobblestone, blocks are useful and decorative. Whenever you see something new, mine it and learn what it's used for.

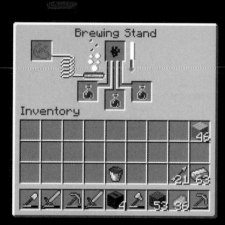

BREWING

As you start to get comfortable with the game, you'll want to look into setting up a brewing station. This is how you brew potions that can have a plethora of effects, from healing to poison and everything in between. Turn them into splash potions by brewing a piece of gunpowder with your potion, then throw them at enemies! These will affect any mobs or players unlucky enough to be caught in the area.

BUILDING

Building is at the heart of Minecraft. Whether it's making a 1x1 tower to escape from a cave or a glorious beachside villa, placing blocks and building will quickly become second nature. Make sure that you've always got a lot of cobblestone on you for use in emergency circumstances!

CAVING

When you find a huge, expansive cave to explore, you better prepare because you can be spelunking in these beauties for ages. Exploring caves is your best shot at killing hostile mobs, earning XP, and finding those elusive diamonds.

COAL

Coal is one of the most important resources in Minecraft. When exploring caves and during the night, it's required for making torches to stop hostile mobs from spawning. It's also the main fuel for use in smelting, which opens up all sorts of possibilities.

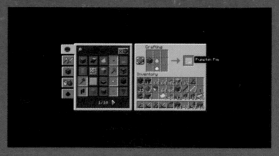

COMBAT

Mastering the unique combat system in Minecraft will take some time, but when you've had some practice with the multiple weapons available and learned how to do things like block and execute critical hits, you'll be on the track to becoming a pro.

CRAFTING

Crafting is a core mechanic in Minecraft and you won't get anywhere without your trusty crafting bench made out of four wooden planks. From there, you can craft anything, from a diamond sword to a delicious pumpkin pie!

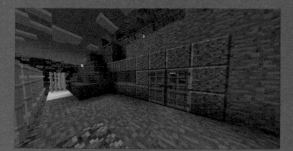

DECORATION

What's the point in building a base if you can't style it to your own unique tastes? There's all sorts of decorative items available, like banners, stained glass, carpets, item frames . . . The list goes on. What are you waiting for? Go and make your house a home!

DIAMONDS

Diamonds are the ultimate find for all Minecraft spelunkers, because they're required for the strongest armor and tools in the game. They're found only at the bottom of the world, though, and usually near lava, so you'd better start mining!

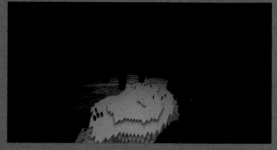

ENCHANTING

When you've set up shop somewhere safe and you've got a full set of tools, weapons, and armor, you can think about enchanting your gear. This makes it even stronger and adds a variety of buffs, but you'll need to farm a lot of XP to enchant everything.

END

There's no ending to Minecraft per se, but the End is another dimension with the toughest boss in the game; the Ender Dragon. It takes a lot of work to reach the End, as you need to visit the Nether and find a stronghold first, but the rewards are worth it!

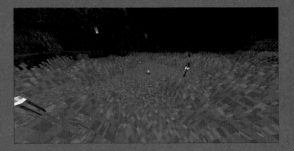

EXPERIENCE POINTS (XP)

Whenever you kill a mob, mine some resources, smelt something in a furnace, or do one of the many other Minecraft actions, you'll earn some experience points. They look like multicolored orbs on the floor and are vital to the enchanting process.

FARMING

Everyone needs to eat! A great source of food can be found by setting up a farm, which can either be focused on crops or animals. From beef to beetroot and pork to potatoes, there's numerous types of food to satiate your hunger in Minecraft.

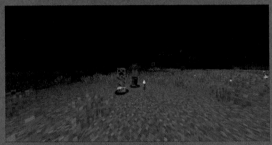

FOOD

You need food to stay healthy, and while you can focus on farms when you have an established base, at the start you need to focus on staying alive. Cows, chickens, pigs, and more will all drop meat for you to cook and can be found commonly on the surface.

HOSTILE MOBS

Mobs is a catch-all term for the creatures you'll find while exploring—and some of them are out to kill you. From the infamous creeper to the flying phantom, get your sword and shield at the ready to take down these formidable foes.

MINING

If caving is wearing you down due to the hostile mobs or you can't find a suitable cave nearby, consider making your own mineshaft near your base. This way, you can search for diamonds and other ores in a systematic fashion and avoid enemies.

NETHER

When you have a diamond pickaxe, you can mine obsidian and create a portal to the Nether. This is a dimension with unique mobs, blocks, and items. If your goal is to reach the End and slay the Ender Dragon, then this is a necessary, albeit dangerous venture.

ORES

While exploring underground, you'll also come across resources known as ores—ideal for crafting tools and armor. Ores look like stone blocks but have colored specks in them. There are two important ones at the start of your game: Coal has black specks, while iron looks brown. There's plenty more to find under the surface though, such as lapus lazuli, gold, diamond, redstone, emerald, and more.

PEACEFUL MOBS

Unlike hostile mobs, peaceful mobs are those that won't attack you—we're talking about sheep, cows, and squid to name a few. It might feel bad, but you'll get some unique and useful items if you kill them. Some of these creatures can also be tamed, such as horses and llamas.

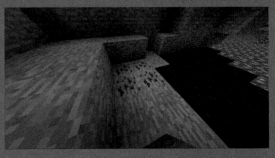

REALMS

If you want to play Minecraft with some friends, you can look into playing on a Realm. The first month is completely free, and it gives you a private and customizable server to use for up to 10 players. There's even a bunch of minigames to try!

REDSTONE

Redstone is a material that can only be found deep below the world's surface, and it's very complicated stuff. It's essentially the same as wiring, and can be used to connect things like levers and buttons to doors and pistons.

SMELTING

You can't do much with unsmelted ores, and raw meat won't help you much compared to the cooked variety! To cook or smelt you'll need a furnace. This can be crafted from eight cobblestone and allows you to smelt all sorts of ores and items.

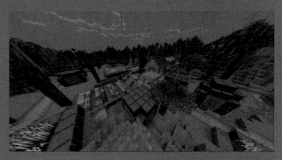

STRUCTURES

You may be the only person in your single player world, but there's plenty of unnatural structures to be found. Abandoned mineshafts and villages are fairly common at the start and there's also ocean monuments, End cities, strongholds, and more.

TOOLS

Unless you simply want to wander the surface like a digital nomad, you'll need to craft the correct tools. You'll need a pickaxe, shovel, and an axe to begin with, followed by more niche tools such as a hoe, shears, and flint and steel later down the line.

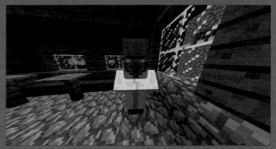

TRADING

Villages are inhabited by the chatty villagers, and you can trade with most of them. Emeralds are the main currency in the world of Minecraft, which can only be found naturally in mountain biomes, and you can both buy and sell items to villagers in exchange for emeralds.

VEHICLES

You can't build a car, but there are vehicles you can craft. Boats carry you across the ocean much faster, while a minecart will carry you across land – as long as it's on rails. You can also take to the skies with the elytra wings, which are an incredibly rare endgame item.

WEAPONS

There's three weapons you'll need to help you slay your foes along the way. The first is a sword—a Minecraft weapon that's useful for any situation. You'll need to make a shield too, to deflect incoming hits. Finally, pick up a bow and arrows to deal serious ranged damage.

. . . AND DON'T MISS

100% UNOFFICIAL!
GAMES MASTER PRESENTS

STAY ALIVE IN MINECRAFT

TIPS FOR DEFEATING CREEPERS, SPIDERS, MONSTERS, AND MORE!

INSIDE YOU WILL FIND

DETAILED DIARIES | BRILLIANT BUILDS | COOL CREATURES | TOP TIPS & TRICKS

ESCAPE FROM VILLAINS

SURVIVE 'TIL THE END

PLAN YOUR ATTACKS

CREATE COOL DEFENSES

The world of Minecraft is full of wonder, discovery, and most of all, fun! But it can also be dangerous, even for the most battle-hardened players. This book will keep you one step ahead of all the mobs and creepers who might try to bring your adventures to a deadly end.

■ Tips and tricks to stay safe in Minecraft   ■ 100% unofficial!

CREATE CRAZY STRUCTURES

EXPERIMENT WITH NATURE

TAKE TO THE SKIES

MAKE MEDIEVAL MASTERPIECES

100% UNOFFICIAL!
GAMES MASTER PRESENTS

COOL BUILDS IN MINECRAFT

50 COOL PROJECTS ANYONE CAN BUILD!

INSIDE YOU WILL FIND

TOP MINI-BUILDS | AWESOME ADVICE | COOL IDEAS | FUN THEMES

The world of Minecraft is full of wonder, discovery, and most of all, fun! Inside this book, you'll find the must-have info on mining resources and creating buildings, vehicles, and entire worlds. Discover everything you need to know from crafting your first shelter to putting the finishing touches on your very own mega-builds.

■ Step-by-step instructions for 50 cool Minecraft builds   ■ 100% unofficial!